More Than Conquerors In Cultural Clashes

RICK DEIGHTON

Carpenter's Son Publishing

More Than Conquerors in Cultural Clashes

© 2020 Rick Deighton

Published by Carpenter's Son Publishing, Franklin, Tennessee

Published in association with Larry Carpenter of Christian Book Services, LLC
www.christianbookservices.com

Cover Design by Paul Sudhakar

Interior Design by Suzanne Lawing

Printed in the United States of America

978-1-949572-90-2

Rick Deighton

Rick Deighton is a graduate of Boise Bible College and later did post-graduate study at Ozark Christian College. After college, Rick served as minister in Eugene, Oregon, for four years. Following that, Rick and his wife, Della, established Alpine Christian Mission, and they served as missionaries in Germany for seven years, working with both the German people and American military stationed there. Since returning to the U. S., Rick has been a bi-vocational missionary for many years, having established a commercial lighting service company. During the past 21 years, he has made multiple mission trips to the former Soviet nations of Estonia, Latvia and Ukraine, which began with an invitation from Reggie Thomas (White Fields Overseas Evangelism). The Deighton's portion of the mission is called Overseas Outreach. Rick has had the privilege of teaching creation evangelism and Biblical worldview in many universities and schools and churches, and even teaching young people on the grounds of a former communist camp. Rick's articles, tracts, booklets and books have been published in English, German, Korean, Georgian, Ukrainian, Turkish and Russian. Rick has also served as Northwest representative of Peace on Earth Ministries. Recently, the Deighton's retired from the lighting business in order to devote more time to vital ministries.

Contents

CHAPTER 1

Why is this Book Needed?

Fighting for America's Soul

To start off answering the question of why this book is needed, I want to share a page from the book, *Fighting For America's Soul*, by Robert H. Knight, published in 2009:

> "…When lawmakers talk confidently about shutting down conservative and Christian talk radio with a re-invented 'Fairness Doctrine,' something is deeply wrong. When activists predict that the United States armed forces will shortly be welcoming open homosexuality, putting women in combat, and that a civilian 'draft' would include our daughters, something is deeply wrong.
>
> But these things do not have to happen. Americans have rallied to enormous challenges, from surviving the Depression to winning two world wars and the Cold War, and assisting with disaster relief on every continent. America also sends missionaries all over the world, bringing the light and love of Jesus Christ into very dark places.
>
> Despite some faults, America has served as the world's economic engine and the beacon of hope for oppressed people

everywhere. The American dream is sustained by the idea that individuals are of inestimable value because they are created in the image of God, with God-given 'unalienable' rights that cannot be abridged by government nor created by government. Through hard work, Americans can achieve whatever they set out to do, unbound by the kind of caste system, religious superstition, and brutal authorities that have prevented human progress elsewhere around the globe.

Free people govern themselves through free enterprise, families, churches, community associations, and charities. The Founders based the U.S. Constitution on Christian principles at the heart of English Common Law, which takes into account man's fallen nature. The Constitution deliberately limits and divides the federal government so that power will not become centralized and tyrannical. At least, that was the plan.

But what was envisioned as a check on government has become a blank check in the hands of unscrupulous judges, legislators, bureaucrats, and presidents. Before our very eyes, we are seeing government become Provider, Judge, and Possessor of All Authority. In short, government is becoming a secular god to which all will be called to kneel – or face sanctions..." (*Fighting for America's Soul: How Sweeping Change Threatens Our Nation and What We Must Do*, Robert H. Knight, 2009 Coral Ridge Ministries Media, Inc. Used by permission.)

Transition from 2009 to 2019

Now I'll transition to 2019 with an issue that is currently in the news and on the minds and hearts of Americans and the entire world. I call it:

"What Green New Deal?"

Recently while waiting for good friends at a Shari's restaurant in Eugene, Oregon, I heard the hauntingly beautiful melody of the sad, sad song, "The Green, Green Grass of Home." The song is about the dream of a prisoner visiting his home once again, then waking up to the reality of the four grey walls of his prison cell on death row. The only green, green grass of home that he could then anticipate would be the sod on his grave – where he would be laid beneath the green, green grass of home after execution for his crime.

As I reflected on the message of that song, I was reminded of the fact that some of our politicians have proposed a "green new deal" that will put America many trillions of dollars deeper in debt – which leaves the major burden to our children, grandchildren and great-grand-children. Why? I confess that I believe the so-called "benefits" of this "green new deal" would be similar to the criminal's dream of seeing and experiencing the green, green grass of home, then waking up to the reality of his crime, his punishment and the green sod of his own grave. The reality of the "green new deal" is the fact that there can be no actual benefits of reducing "greenhouse gases" unless China, India and multitudes of other nations choose to cooperate. Add to this the fact that the sun would have to cooperate with the wild plan of social-ist politicians because sunspots and explosions on the sun have far more effect on climate change than anything puny human beings are doing (or not doing). The reality is that our children and grandchil-dren will be buried under the fraud of this socialist scam like millions of other poor people have been for over 100 years in socialist nations around the globe.

The Reality About Climate Change

I serve on the leadership team for Museum of Truth. Our field paleontologist, Stan Lutz, told me that for as long as humans have recorded climate change (about 150 years), there has been fluctuation between global warming and global cooling. Some of us still remem-ber back when the scare tactics were about another ice age coming upon us. (If you want to verify fluctuating climate change, you can contact Stan through our contact information on p. 235.)

I am not a government employee, but I did write my original

thoughts with a green pen – on my own time. This was not done at government expense, and I didn't charge the government $1,000,000 for a green pen!

My hope of the green, green grass of Home is not the beautiful green grass of Eugene, where Della and I lived for four years, where Randy was born and where we adopted Sandy, nor the green grass of my hometown, Longmont, Colorado, nor of Boise, where Della and I met, married and began our home together. No! **My hope is in Jesus Christ and His righteousness. He is trustworthy! He fulfills His promises! My green, green grass of Home will be my eternal Home – on the New Earth in my new body (resurrection style)! Want to join me? Put your trust in Jesus – He will not disappoint you!**

Pertinent Perspective About Why This Book is Needed

Next, here is a copy of Tim Wildmon's August 2019 letter to supporters of American Family Association:

"I admit that I don't understand the 'progressive' mind.

When public libraries – in the name of tolerance and diversity – invite transvestite 'drag queens' to read to a group of children – I am NOT sympathetic.

Check out the photo that is Los Angeles drag queen Xochi Mochi reading to children at the Long Beach public library at an event called 'Drag Queen Story Hour.' The drag queen at the Lansdale, Pennsylvania library even used the name 'Annie Christ.'" (Get it? I'm sure you do.)

Even as I write this, I feel my anger rising.

THESE ARE CHILDREN!

I wish this insanity represented isolated events, but it does not. *First Things,* a respected publication, reports that Drag Queen Story Hours are a 'global phenomenon' with more than 35 chapters in the U.S. alone, and that the events often draw hundreds of participants.

The *New York Times* defended these abominations as 'nice public event[s].' *Slate* magazine called them mere exhibitions of 'free speech and association.' A writer for *Reason* said Christians who object to Drag Queen Story Hours are nothing more than 'some sort of theocratic street squad that terrorizes librarians who invite drag queens to read to kids.'

And the madness doesn't stop there.

From the world of pro-death politics, U.S. Senator Kirsten Gillibrand (D-NY), one of 24 Democrats running for their party's presidential nomination, told the Des Moines Register (Iowa) newspaper that judges who might overturn *Roe v Wade*, the 1973 Supreme Court ruling that legalized abortion, were 'ultra-radical conservative[s]' who were no different from 'a judge who's racist or anti-Semitic or homophobic.'

The Senator went on to arrogantly state that while she 'respect[s] the rights of Americans to hold religious beliefs true to themselves,' there was no legitimate 'other side' to these kinds of issues.

In other words, there is the godless, leftist, Marxist way of thinking about moral issues, and nothing else should be tolerated!

And she wants to be president!

Christians, we are in a war with evil. God help us remain faithful and ready to defend the truths of Scripture.

To that end, AFA is committed to providing helpful resources like the video presentation offered on the enclosed gift slip. It's titled **Worldviews: Behaviors, Beliefs, and Values**. The presentation features author, speaker, and radio host Alex McFarland.

Let there be no doubt that the intent of these far-left extremists is pure evil. Consider these recent attempts to radicalize our children and grandchildren:

Arthur (PBS) – In May, the beloved animated children's series revealed that one of its longtime main characters and Arthur's teacher, Mr. Ratburn, is 'gay' and getting married. The episode was titled, 'Mr. Ratburn and the Special Someone.'

Cartoon Network – For LGBTQ Pride Month in June, the popular children's network tweeted out the message: 'We want to wish everyone a HAPPY PRIDE and encourage all of our LGBTQ+ fans to stand proud all year long!' The tweet carried a picture of characters from the animated series Powerpuff Girls.

My Little Pony – Also in June, popular Discovery Family network series, *My Little Pony: Friendship is Magic,* debuted a same sex couple on the episode 'The Last Crusade.' Just to make sure their relationship was clear, Michael Vogel, a writer and producer for the series, tweeted that the two ponies were, in fact, a lesbian couple.

These purveyors of evil don't care what parents and grandparents think. They are aiming for our children.

And their propaganda storm has already eroded much of the moral bedrock of our nation, as a Gallup survey in May found.

Gallup research consultant Megan Brenan wrote in an analysis, '[Approval of] sex between an unmarried man and woman is at its highest point in the Gallup trend.'

The poll also found that 63% of survey respondents said that gay and lesbian relationships were morally acceptable, a 23% increase in the last 18 years.

The Gallup research also confirmed what most thinking people already know: 'Americans' perspectives on the morality of different behaviors are strongly influenced by their own ideology.' In other words, your worldview determines what you think is morally acceptable or unacceptable.

Participants in the poll identifying as 'very liberal/liberal' approved of abortion, homosexual relationships, fornication, and pornography over those who were 'very conservative/conservative' by margins of 50, 36, 33 and 30 percentage points, respectively.

This clearly demonstrates two critical realities for America going forward: 1) Christians must be instructed about what the Bible teaches and what it means for our nation's moral foundations; and 2) Christians must be salt and light – including being active in culture and politics.

If Christians abandon the battlefield, these immoral radicals will vote their values and 'evangelize' our children and grandchildren to their godless worldview.

The souls of our nation AND our children are at stake.

As you know, for more than four decades AFA has been in this fight because we love God's church, we love America, and we love our families.

May we never lose our grip on that vision, nor cease to battle the forces of wickedness that seek to destroy it.

How do we go forward in that vision? First, we must recognize that ideas have consequences. In other words, a nation impacted by Christianity is going to look much different than one dominated by a Marxist, Muslim, or other worldview.

Then, we must learn to defend and articulate the truth of a Christian worldview in contrast to the myriad of other belief systems in the world.

And my friend Alex McFarland, the host of **Worldviews: Behaviors, Beliefs, and Values**, is just the person to help us do that. Alex came to headquarters in Tupelo, just to film this presentation for AFA supporters.

In 2 Chronicles 20:15, three armies were moving toward the certain destruction of Jerusalem. Then King Jehoshaphat prayed, and the Lord answered with these words:

> *Do not be afraid and do not be dismayed at this*
> *great horde, for the battle is not yours but God's.*
> *Tomorrow go down against them. … Stand firm, hold your*
> *position, and see the salvation of the Lord on your behalf.*

At AFA, we face God's enemies with the full knowledge that the battle is His. And yet, it is our privilege and duty to 'go down against' the forces aligned against Him.

For the cause of Christ, our King,
Tim Wildmon, AFA President"

Taken from Gallup's annual Values and Beliefs poll that tracks American's views on 21 moral issues Source: news.gallup.com, May 29, 2019			
MORAL ACCEPTABILITY OF ISSUES BY IDEOLOGY	Very conservative/ Conservative	Very liberal/liberal	Difference
Gay or lesbian relationships	45%	81%	36%
Abortion	23%	73%	50%
Sex between unmarried man and woman	54%	87%	33%
Pornography	23%	53%	30%

Liberal and Logical?

Have you noticed that the word "liberal" in contemporary usage does not seem to fit with the word "logical"? For example, there are "liberal" politicians who are vowing to take our guns away (in violation of our 2nd amendment to the Constitution). Why? They say it's to protect us from more mass shootings. Really? When you criminalize gun ownership, then only criminals will have guns! Criminals have already demonstrated that they are not law-abiding citizens, so how logical is it to believe that criminals with murderous intensions are going to surrender their guns and ammunition? Are you aware that very often a murderous assault has been stopped by a law-abiding citizen with a gun? These are the heroes among us! So "liberals" want to disarm the heroes and give the criminals free access to slaughter everyone in their path in schools, shopping malls, etc.? Logical and liberal? Hmmm!

Do liberals know just a little American history? The reason for the 2nd amendment is not for us to have guns for hunting, target practice, etc. Our founding fathers for this amazing country knew history, and they were intent on American citizens being able to protect themselves from an overreaching government that would become the persecuting criminal. The Nazis had citizens of Germany register their guns, then turn in their guns. So did the communists – in country after country. So, who are the "liberals"? Are they the protectors - or the criminals?

Oh, yes. I also heard recently of an individual who viciously attacked many people with a knife. So, are "liberals" going to ban our knives?

How are butcher shops, restaurant kitchens, and housewives going to do their work without knives? This morning I heard report about a teen who attacked another teen with a frying pan! Are "liberals" going to protect us by banning pans? "Liberal" and logical? Hmmm?

Actually, even though the words "liberal" and "criminal" don't begin with the same letter, they do rhyme! Hmmm! Just thinking!

Of course, if the "liberal" is actually a Marxist, whose goal is to destroy this constitutional republic in order to fundamentally change it into a socialist dictatorship in which the government is in control of everything and everybody, then it is logical to do what he's doing. Logical – and criminal! (I mean criminal, as in treason.) I mean criminal, as in following the Marxist mantra that the end justifies the means; that is, that you can call evil good and good evil if it advances your cause. You can make up lies to accuse a President or Supreme Court Justice if that advances your cause. You can adamantly promote the slaughter of innocent babies in the womb (and even after they survive a botched abortion) if that advances your cause. You can cover up the atrocities of abortionists with filthy, unsanitary conditions in their butcher shops where the deluded women who enter are also victims along with the babies they slaughter. You can continue to promote the pornography in the classrooms perpetrated by Planned Parenthood under the guise of sex education. You can continue to also try to cover up the genocide of black babies perpetrated by Margaret Sanger, founder of Planned Parenthood and continued to this day by that infamous organization. You can continue to try to siphon off millions of our tax dollars for the slaughter of the unborn citizens of America if it promotes your cause. You can make movies and TV programs that promote perverts like Alfred Kinsey, who molested little children in his experiments and interviewed criminals in his research in order to promote the lie that ten percent of our population are practicing sodomy. You can promote him and other perverts as heroes if you so choose, because it fits your agenda, but beware – your sin will find you out! *"For we must all appear before the judgment seat of Christ, that each one may receive the things done in the body, according to what he has done, whether good or bad."* 2 Corinthians 5:10

Do you feel that I'm speaking too strongly? I agree that these are strong words, but the stench of the filth of abortion butcher shops and the outrage of cover-up programs in Congress and on campaign trails is even much worse. When David Daleiden and his co-workers are being charged as criminals because they exposed the atrocities of Planned Parenthood, then the real criminals need to be exposed. Are you disturbed about what is happening to our beloved country? Are you outraged? If no, why not? As Charles H. Spurgeon said back in the 1800's about evolutionism, "The time for soft speaking is over!" Years ago, at one of the "Man and the Christian Worldview Symposiums" where I was a presenter, one of the interpreters said, "One thing about Rick – you never have to wonder what he is trying to say!" So, if you want to read the work of an author who is so vague you can't tell what he really believes, this book is not for you!

I do want to speak the truth in love, as the Word of God teaches, but I also notice in Scripture that sometimes love must be tough. Jesus is our ultimate example, and I realize that sometimes He was consumed with the zeal of His Father, as when He drove out the money changers from the temple and used strong, even scathing words of condemnation against the religious leaders of His nation when exposing their hypocrisy and denouncing their corruption. (See Matthew chapter 23.)

Usually I like to be as uplifting and affirming as possible, so here are my wishes for you who read these words and choose to follow our Savior (whether you agree with me or not on all my convictions):

"Now may the God of hope fill you with all joy and peace as you trust in Him, so that you may overflow with hope by the power of the Holy Spirit." Romans 15:13

May Almighty God continue to expand your godly influence for His glory!

May the resurrected Lord Jesus be always your joy, your hope, your comfort, your strength and victory! May you come to know Him deeper, love Him dearer, and follow Him nearer!

"The Lord your God in your midst, the Mighty One will save; He will rejoice over you with gladness, He will quiet you in His love, He will rejoice over you with singing." Zephaniah 3:17

Why This Book is Needed – Continued

Now to round out my reply to why this book is needed, I'm sharing with you the initial pages of the book *More than Conquerors in Cultural Clashes* as it was first published by Search for the Truth Ministries in 2013 and republished by WestBow Press in 2016.

Reviewer Comment by Reggie Thomas

"When your first chapter arrived I decided that even though I am now packing and making last minute preparations to fly to Haiti that I would take the time to read Chapter one. It was interesting, inspiring, and challenging to read it. You have done an excellent job, as usual, in writing a very scholarly chapter, as well as an easy reading chapter. I tried to read it as an unbeliever seeking information. Reading it this way, I can tell you truthfully that I was tremendously challenged and helped to believe in the truth of God's Word, as opposed to the false fairy tales of unbelievers. I only offer one suggestion for improvement. In the early part of the chapter as you presented a very brief appeal to the lost sinner to find salvation in Jesus, I think it was too brief. I suggest you give a fuller, more complete presentation of the plan of salvation here. Later on in the chapter your own personal testimony is a powerful presentation and very convincing. If in the earlier part you gave a complete presentation of the plan of salvation, then I think when the reader reaches your own personal testimony, it would be even more powerful."

In Christian love, Reggie

~

"I know I have previously sent you my thoughts on Chapter I, but after re-reading I want to add two thoughts:

1). You mention that you fear that you are so eager to get your message across that you may come across too strong or too passionate and without enough love. Rick, dismiss this fear from your mind. After re-reading chapter 1, I can testify that I never felt more Christian love than I felt coming from your pen!

2). Reading Sandy's Appendix brought tears to my eyes as I felt more than ever the Christian love coming through your pen and from Sandy's heartfelt testimony.

In Christian love, Reggie

Dedication

I want to begin this dedication with a confession – that I neglected to put a dedication in our second published book. Yes, my name is on the cover, but I often say "our books" because they would not exist without Della. When God gave me a helper (helpmate), He gave me the perfect fit to help me transfer my thoughts scratched out on scratch paper, backs of envelopes, etc. to a clear, legible form. Since our college days Della has faithfully typed and transformed my scribbling into theme papers, tracts, booklets and now two books prior to *More Than Conquerors in Cultural Clashes*. I gave a small dedication to Della in *Ready to Give an Answer*, but *Is the Bible Without Any Errors?* should have been dedicated to Della also. I neglected to give credit where credit is due and honor to whom honor is due. I confess my negligence and ask your forgiveness, Della Lu. I love you, Della Lu, and I thank God for you. So belatedly I dedicate the first two books to you.

Now, however, we both agree that the dedication for *More Than Conquerors in Cultural Clashes* is to Sandy Joy, our office manager for both Deighton Lighting and Overseas Outreach, but more importantly, our own adopted daughter. We have loved you from the first moment we saw your picture as a sweet three-month-old baby, then as we actually held you as our own at eight months. We have watched you grow in wisdom and stature (to all of 5'1"), taught you to love Jesus, baptized you, and observed you as you handled rejection and deep grief with grace and forgiveness (as a shining example to us and others). Your sweet spirit comes through in such a warm, pleasant, friendly manner when you pick up the phone and say, "Deighton Lighting – this is Sandy." Your people skills with customers, friends, and Idaho Power representatives are not inferior to your office skills with typing, computer, internet and organizing files of information. I really meant it when I told you recently about the book, "I couldn't be doing this without you." So, *More Than Conquerors in Cultural Clashes* is dedicated to Sandra Joy (Deighton) Smith. God has richly endowed you with the gifts and abilities to complement and enhance the way He has gifted each of us – all to His honor and glory. We thank God for you – deeply and sincerely!

Now, readers, I should also rightly mention that Sandy helped a great deal with *Is the Bible Without Any Errors?* in preparing it for publication. *Ready to Give an Answer* was published before she came to work for us.

As an additional note – we have been asked if it is possible to love an adopted child as much as our own biological child. (Randy is our son – we love him deeply.) To answer this question, I want to clarify that Sandy's temperament, personality and skills are so similar to Della's that some people say she's a duplicate, although she doesn't look exactly like Della. Once Della said to Sandy, "Well, you probably inherited that from me." Sandy replied, "Mom! I wasn't born from you!" Della responded, "Oh, yeah. I forgot!"

If you are considering adoption, we highly recommend it. It is a wonderful option! You may rescue a child for Jesus and discover that He blesses you abundantly with a lifelong co-worker and companion for life's journey. Also, your adopted child may become the source of the fun and frolic of beautiful grandchildren!

Unique Perspective

I believe God has prepared me for years to write this book from a unique perspective. In fact, this may be the major reason why God gave me life and put me here on this earth. In our August prayer letter for Overseas Outreach I wrote: *"Please pray for publication of "More Than Conquerors in Cultural Clashes" soon. We have now finished the manuscript except for some finishing touches, refining from suggestions for improvement by our reviewers, and waiting for permissions to quote. My prayer is that this book will challenge, inspire, and encourage fellow believers to stand up, straighten up and speak up for Jesus, while demolishing strongholds of deception and degradation. Will you pray with me for God to use this book as a spark for revival and spiritual awakening?"*

Here are a few reasons why I believe God has uniquely prepared me for this task:

1. God placed in my heart a love for reading when I was still a child, so I have been reading widely since I was a youth.

2. I grew up in a mixed family. My mother was a nominal believer and sent me to Bible classes, but my father, older brother, and all my uncles on my father's side were atheists, agnostics, evolutionists, and Biblical skeptics. At a very young age I declared myself an atheist when I said, "I don't believe in God! I've never seen Him!" I am so thankful that God by His amazing grace, and through a dramatic answer to my first earnest, personal prayer, drew me out of that web of unbelief into His kind, loving arms.

3. When I was a senior in high school, I read *Masters of Deceit*, by J. Edgar Hoover, former director of the FBI, as a project for a book report. It was an insightful look at the deceptive tactics

of Marxism. This foundation has given me a clear perception of what has been happening in our nation for so many years. I'm appalled that many Americans seem to be so ignorant of Marxism that they don't recognize it in our schools, universities, journals, and government offices all the way to the Supreme Court, Congress, and the White House.

Ronald Reagan once quipped:
"Who is a communist?
- someone who reads Marx and Engles.
Who is an anti-communist?
- someone who understands Marx and Engles!"

4. I've had an excellent foundation in Bible, Theology, Apologetics, Philosophy, Preaching and Teaching Ministry, Missions, and Writing Ministry at Boise Bible College and Ozark Bible College.

5. While in my fifth year of Bible College I read *None Dare Call it Treason,* and wrote an essay about it for a contest. Although I did not win the first prize I had hoped for, I did win a prize and learned valuable information.

6. While preparing to go to Germany as a missionary and church planter, I served for four years (1966-1970) as preaching minister for a church in Eugene, Oregon – between Seattle and San Francisco on Interstate Hwy. I-5. This was during the extreme turbulence of campus riots and the rise of the hippie movement. Reaching out to students on the University of Oregon campus was as much a continuing education for me as it was effective evangelism for touching them.

7. We founded Alpine Christian Mission and served seven years doing outreach in Germany and Switzerland. Learning to understand and relate to German/Western European mentality was also a continuing education.

8. I have served as Missions Professor for one year at Boise Bible

College, as well as serving as associate minister of preaching at a local church.

9. For over thirty years I've served as a bi-vocational missionary, and we founded Overseas Outreach after being invited by Reggie Thomas to serve with him as an associate evangelist for White Fields Overseas Evangelism. For the past fifteen years I've observed firsthand the devastation of Marxism /Evolutionism in former Soviet Union nations.

10. We own and operate our own business, Deighton Lighting (I'm not good at sewing, so I didn't try tent making. Besides, this way I get to share the Light all the time).

11. I've taught Christian Evidences in camps in Estonia and churches in Latvia. I've taught a one-week modular course in Christian Evidences and Creation Science and Evangelism at Zaparozia Bible College in Ukraine, and repeatedly for Tavrisky Christian Institute in Ukraine and Georgia.

12. Sergei Golovin invited me to come to Crimea as a presenter for the "Man and the Christian Worldview Symposium" in the spring of 2001. God opened many doors and I have taught at these symposiums and Creation Conferences for about twelve years. Now I often teach "Worldview" and "Building Lasting Relationships" lessons on both Christian and secular campuses in Ukraine.

13. As of December 14, 2012, Della and I have been married for fifty years. This gives some credibility to teaching on "Building Lasting Relationships" and for my chapter, "Phony Matrimony vs. Merry Marriage."

14. Bruce Malone of Search for the Truth Ministries has published my (our) two former books, *Ready to Give an Answer* and *Is the Bible Without Any Errors?* We have confirmation that they are touching hearts and lives of readers, - not only English readers,

but Russian and Georgian as well.

15. Reggie Thomas, Founder of White Fields Overseas Evangelism and a living legend in missions and church planting worldwide, has gladly agreed to write the introduction for *More than Conquerors in Cultural Clashes.*

16. I served as associate minister with Gary Strubhar in Gresham, Oregon, and he has graciously reviewed the manuscript for *More than Conquerors in Cultural Clashes.* Recently he wrote concerning Chapter 6:

"Dear Fellow Kingdom Co-worker,

Rick, you are a bold witness and author! You are spot-on with your analysis of the current 'mess we are in.' You have the facts and the truth from Scripture, applied timely to the enemy's strategies. Please reserve several copies of your coming new book. Every soldier in the Lord's army needs the information in chapter 6! (yes, 1-6) Bold, winsome, wise, witnesses are so needed in today's culture. You are truly a bold, Spirit-filled witness, and author. You represent the heart of God just as the O.T. prophets did. Bless you for your zeal. The 'world' is truly the enemy of the Cross. We are facing bold spiritual warfare and it's past time that every serious believer gets informed and bold about the issues at hand. We are the Light of the world. If we are dim lights, we influence nobody. But when we are bold and not timid, those who oppose us will know they are in 'darkness' whether or not they admit it. Gary S."

Would you consider partnering with us to give *More than Conquerors in Cultural Clashes* a wide distribution to Americans?

Personal Motivation

If you are reading the book alone, the questions can help motivate you to actually study, remember, and apply the lessons in order to become a more active and bold witness for our Lord Jesus Christ. I offer you the opportunity – in fact, I challenge you – **to get serious**

about gaining confidence to be who you are in Christ. Are you winning in the spiritual battle going on inside you? Are you making a positive difference in the cultural clashes in our country? In your county? In your city? In your own family? If not– why not? Do you really want to hear our Commander in Chief say to you, 'Well done, good and faithful servant!"? Are you living and serving as a good soldier of our Lord Jesus, or are you a coward? Are you AWOL in the heat of the battle? This book can help you, and Jesus can transform you if you are willing, but only you can supply the personal motivation and application. What will you do? If you just shake your head and say, "What is this world coming to?" – you missed the point! This world is going to hell! You already knew that! What are you doing to rescue as many souls as possible from that pit? That is the question. Transformation of our nation will happen one soul at a time!

Here is my wish for all of you: *"May the God of hope fill you with all joy and peace as you trust in him, so that you may overflow with hope by the power of the Holy Spirit."* Romans 15:13 (NIV)

How do You Handle Criticism?
(Humbly Listening or Proudly Rejecting?)

Ravi Zacharias tells of a furious man he knew who came storming out of a counseling session and asked him: "Do you know what he said to me? He said that I don't handle criticism well!" Need I comment?

In the same broadcast, Ravi quipped, "The depravity of man is the most easily verifiable truth – but the most strongly resisted." He illustrated this with an example of a reaction he got from a woman in an academic setting. During the question session following his presentation, an irate lady with a shrill voice was strongly opposing Ravi's point about human beings having a flawed nature – as the Word of God teaches. Jeremiah 17:9 says, *"The heart is deceitful above all things, and desperately wicked; who can know it?"* As she became more intense with her argument, her anger became more evident, her face more red and her voice more shrill, Ravi resisted the temptation to say what he felt like saying – "Sit down and be quiet – you just proved my point!"

Ravi had already presented truth, so he responded with compassion instead of logic. He could have embarrassed her before the whole crowd. I'm not sure I would have resisted that temptation, but in this case, I realize that his compassion was better than logic. I want to be more like this in speaking the truth in love. There is a time to confront – a time to speak – but also a time to be silent. In this case his silence was an act of love while letting the truth already spoken sink in. After all, our purpose is to win people, not arguments.

Friend, how do you handle criticism – by humbly listening or proudly rejecting? Will you be wise enough to honestly, humbly consider these passages from God's wisdom literature?

"He who corrects a scoffer gets shame for himself, and he who rebukes a wicked man only harms himself. Do not correct a scoffer, lest he hate you; rebuke a wise man, and he will love you. Give instruction to a wise man, and he will be still wiser; teach a just man, and he will increase in learning. 'The fear of the Lord is the beginning of wisdom, and the knowledge of the Holy One is understanding'. . .Open rebuke is better than love carefully concealed. Faithful are the wounds of a friend, but the kisses of an enemy are deceitful." Proverbs 9:7-10, 27:5-6

"It is better to hear the rebuke of the wise than for a man to hear the song of fools." Ecclesiastes 7:5

Bottom line note: Some years ago when Alexander Solzhenitsyn spoke to a gathering of Harvard students, warning them of the consequences of adopting Marxism, they mocked him. Were those brilliant students demonstrating wisdom or foolishness? Remember that intelligence and wisdom are not the same. You can have a head full of information and a heart full of rebellion and foolishness. I remember my Dad speaking of the "educated fools" – those with a bushel of information without a thimble full of practical good sense (no wisdom of how to use it).

Were the Leaders of Israel and Rome in Jesus' Time Wise

Is it possible to accumulate information (knowledge, science) while at the same time crucifying Truth and Wisdom? The religious leaders of Israel in Jesus' time had a vast accumulation of Biblical and secular knowledge, yet they manipulated the crucifixion of Truth Himself.

Jesus had said to the religious leaders: *"You search the Scriptures, for in them you think you have eternal life; and these are they which testify of Me."* John 5:39

Some years after Jesus' death, burial and resurrection, the apostle Paul wrote, *"However, we speak wisdom among those who are mature, yet not the wisdom of this age, nor of the rulers of this age, who are coming to nothing. But we speak the wisdom of God in a mystery, the hidden wisdom which God ordained before the ages for our glory, which none of the rulers of this age knew; for had they known, they would not have crucified the Lord of glory."* 1 Corinthians 2:6-8

Foreword by Gary Strubhar

*Retired minister, college professor, elder, servant with
40 years of kingdom fellowship with the Deighton's*

(Note: *Gary was one of my best friends and he wrote this Foreword for the 2013 publication of this book. Now, due to Parkinson's disease, Gary is at Home in Glory with our Lord Jesus Christ.*)

For more than 35 years Thomas Kinkade painted legendary landscapes of light. "Thomas Kinkade, painter of light" became his registered trademark. Rick Deighton may not be as famous as Thomas Kinkade, but Rick is a spreader and promoter of light. The famous painter said every original painting comes from what he first draws.

Rick also draws—conclusions—about our current culture. Doesn't that seem natural, since he built and operates Rick Deighton Lighting? His passion for turning darkness to light is not a new idea; he has lived the life of a light-bearer for decades! I know from working with him - he is not ashamed of Jesus or His message. Rick knows God did not give us a spirit of fear and timidity, but of power, love and sound mind. His kind is especially needed in our generation. He has never met a stranger with whom he couldn't begin a pleasant, positive conversation.

Never in the last 400 years have we witnessed such an attack on Christian morals and values! From Hollywood to your neighborhood, from every government school and college to the local and national media—it's one constant stream of belittling and outright attack on the "Light."

Jesus' words to Nicodemus are equally true now as then: *"This is the crisis we're in: God-light streamed into the world, but men and women everywhere ran for the darkness. They went for the darkness because they were not really interested in pleasing God. Everyone who makes a practice of doing evil, addicted to denial and illusion, hates God-light and won't come near it, fearing a painful exposure. But anyone working and living in truth and reality welcomes God-light so the work can be seen for the God-work it is." [The Message. Jn.3:19-21] The apostle John gives us further light: "He [Jesus] created everything there is. Nothing exists that he didn't make. Life itself was in him, and this life gives light to everyone. The light shines through the darkness, and the darkness can never extinguish it."* [Jn. 1:3-5] And so the crisis continues! Rick's pertinent expose' is more than a reaction to the evils of our day. It is a resource book crammed full of evidence of the decay around us. Dark days are upon us; evil is more tolerated, excused, and even laughed at. Light-bearers are scoffed and scorned and insulted as inferior or ignorant. But remember, modern (and ancient) culture has always opposed the good news of God. The apostle Paul instructs us to *"take no part in the worthless deeds of evil and darkness; instead, rebuke and expose them". This is why it says, 'Wake up from your sleep, climb out of your coffins, Christ will show you the light.'"* [NLT and Message Eph. 5:11-14]

So here's the crisis and here's our assignment. Let Rick Deighton's passion, observations, research, and warnings help shine through your life, words, and witness. Inform yourself and others about the rebellion, the 'tolerance,' the violence, the attack on marriage, purity, and purpose. Rick does a masterful job of integrating Scripture, quotes, illustrations, real-life personal illustrations, and testimonies. All this done in an easy to read, contemporary style. He will remind you of a prophet, and this is what America needs—now. And if you only have time to read part, please read his chapter 4 and his powerful closing remarks.

Commit yourself to the practical action steps in each chapter so we can do more than react—we can be light! *Be no longer inhibited; be inhabited!*

Introduction by Reggie Thomas

(Note: Reggie wrote this for the first publication in 2013.)

It is a wonderful privilege and a great honor to be asked to write the introduction for this particular book "MORE THAN CONQUERORS IN CULTURAL CLASHES" written by my good friend and co-laborer in the Lord, Rick Deighton. In introducing this book please take note of what Chief Justice Roy Moore has written. Judge Moore was sued by the ACLU for displaying the Ten Commandments in his courtroom foyer. He was stripped of his judgeship and removed from the bench for refusing to remove the Ten Commandments from his courtroom. The people of Alabama have re-elected him as Judge for the Supreme Court of Alabama. The following is a poem written by Judge Roy Moore:

> *America the Beautiful,*
> *or so you used to be.*

Land of the Pilgrims' pride;
I'm glad they'll never see.

Babies piled in dumpsters,
Abortion on demand,
Oh, sweet land of liberty;
your house is on the sand.

Our children wander aimlessly
poisoned by cocaine
choosing to indulge their lusts,
when God has said abstain.

From sea to shining sea,
our Nation turns away
From the teaching of God's love
and a need to always pray.

We've kept God in our temples,
how callous we have grown.
When earth is but His footstool,
and Heaven is His throne.

We've voted in a government
that's rotting at the core,
Appointing Godless Judges;
who throw reason out the door,

Too soft to place a killer
in a well deserved tomb,
But brave enough to kill a baby
before he leaves the womb.

You think that God's not angry,
that our land's a moral slum?
How much longer will He wait

before His judgment comes?

How are we to face our God,
from Whom we cannot hide?
What then is left for us to do,
but stem this evil tide?

If we who are His children,
will humbly turn and pray;
Seek His holy face
and mend our evil way:
Then God will hear from Heaven;
and forgive us of our sins,
He'll heal our sickly land
and those who live within.

But, America the Beautiful,
if you don't - then you will see,
A sad but Holy God
withdraw His hand from Thee.
~~Judge Roy Moore~~

This poem by Judge Moore says it all so well. Those of us who are adult Americans never thought things would be as they now are:

*millions of babies murdered by abortion on demand----

*drug addicts by the millions filling our jails and prisons---

*lesbianism and homosexuality approved by our President----

*prayer and Bible reading forbidden in school where condoms are handed out freely---

Yes, our beloved America is sick, and we are in danger of God judging us with fire and brimstone as He did to Sodom and Gomorrah!

Rick Deighton fearlessly exposes the errors, sins, evil and foolish ways of America. Rick is a true scholar and yet he writes in easy to understand ways in PRESENTING TRUTH, DEFENDING TRUTH, AND EXPOSING ERROR. You will love this book because Rick will help you to prepare to be a bold witness for Jesus Christ and to be ready to give clear answers to tough questions. And as you complete reading the book I pray that you will help to spread the news about this marvelous book to all Americans.

In Christian love,

Reggie Thomas, Evangelist,

White Fields Overseas Evangelism

Questions for Chapter 1

1. What impressed you most about the quote by Robert Knight from the 2009 book, *Fighting for America's Soul*?

2. What does the message contained in the sad song, "The Green, Green Grass of Home," have to do with the socialist program plan titled, "What Green New Deal"?

3. What does Rick Deighton share as his hope for the green, green grass of Home?

4. What important truth about climate change did Stan Lutz find in his research?

5. Does it bother you that libraries in various states across our nation are hosting so-called "drag queens" to read propaganda books to children? (If not, I have another question for you – do you still have a pulse?)

6. Does it disturb you (or leave you appalled) by the percentage of those who call themselves Conservatives or Very Conservative – yet are accepting of:

   "Gay" or lesbian relationships

   Abortion

   Sexual immorality between men and women

Pornography?

7. Do you see why our country is in deep, deep trouble and desperately in need of spiritual awakening? What do you plan to do about it?

8. Reggie Thomas wrote both a Reviewer Comment and the Introduction for the original publication of *More than Conquerors in Cultural Clashes*. What was for you the most important observation that Reggie made?

9. I dedicated this book to our daughter, Sandy. Why – and what connection does this have with "the wonderful option of adoption?"

10. Under the title "Unique Perspective," I listed 16 reasons why I believe God has called me and prepared me for the task of writing this book. Did these reasons come across as convincing to your mind and heart? Why or why not?

Bonus Question

What is the purpose of the section titled "Personal Motivation"?

CHAPTER 2:

How Truly Tolerant is the Tolerant Troop?

What is Tolerance?

"Tolerance in our society has come to mean 'give up your way immediately and accept mine or you are a prejudiced bigot' and considered intolerant for not letting the other be intolerant!"
~ D. Lloyd Thomas (Used by permission.)

The question I've used as the title for this chapter is pertinent and relevant because the meaning of the word "tolerance" has changed. If we personify "tolerance" as a woman, she has not only changed a few items in her wardrobe, she has had a complete make- over. Both Josh McDowell and Randy Alcorn have clearly documented and illustrated this radical change of meaning. I want to use portions of an insightful article by Randy Alcorn to clarify this transformation in meaning:

"Same Words – Different Meaning"
"Defining Truth in Postmodern Christianity"

By Randy Alcorn

"...Of course, evangelicalism as a subculture is riddled with any number of failings, and tends to be geared toward a certain audience that can unintentionally exclude postmoderns. These criticisms we should welcome and take seriously and make changes where appropriate. But we dare not throw out the baby of Christian truth with the bathwater of evangelical failings. What's at stake in this issue is not merely different ideas on how we relate to culture or live out and share the faith – what is at stake is the faith itself, historic Christianity.

When it comes to the issue of objective truth, this is where some churches seem to me to be stepping over the line. Truth is an issue of seismic proportions, and if we have eyes to see, it is everywhere around us. Often we don't see it, though, because we can have nice conversations at church in which we assume that those we've talked with meant the same thing we did when they used certain words. But in fact, they didn't.

For instance, a teenager comes home from school. Her Christian parent asks, "What did you learn today"?

After an obligatory mumble, she says, "In social science we talked about the importance of being tolerant."

"That's nice," the parent says. Daughter talks, and you nod, because you know Jesus loved people and extended them grace, and we should too. A few minutes later the conversation is over, and you walk away having affirmed what she learned in class, without understanding the context and meaning of her culture – and the fact that what you actually affirmed was anti-Christian.

Why? Because *tolerant* means two radically different things

to you and to her. To you it means being kind and loving to people who think and act in ways you know to be wrong, according to Scripture. To the students and their teacher – and by assimilation even to your Christian teenager unless she is exceptionally well-grounded in Scripture – tolerant means believing that all ways of thinking and acting are equally valid, and NOT wrong.

By believing Jesus is the only way for people to enter Heaven, you are by definition intolerant. By embracing tolerance, in the sense it is most widely used in this culture, our young people (whether or not they state it and regardless of what their church believes) are rejecting the idea that Jesus is the only way.

There are significantly different meanings out there for the old words *truth, tolerance, love, grace, redemption, salvation* and even *Christ.* Postmodern evangelicalism does not simply invent new words, which would be far better for purposes of clarity – it uses the same old words and attaches to them new meanings, often meanings contradictory to the original.

…The notion that there is no such thing as objective truth – and therefore no objective meaning for words such as the *resurrection* and *grace* – is a natural extension of both our culture's self-preoccupation and mental laziness. It is self-flattery to imagine truth is merely whatever I decide, think, and make of life. It is also laziness. Once people sought truth by going to philosophers and historic religions, now they sit and watch television and simply absorb worldviews without consciously evaluating them.

Everyone has a worldview, but few really seek to find the right one. The myth that there is no right worldview, that all are equally valid, becomes moral justification for believing whatever we wish, and keeps us from seeking further. No one needs to go to the trouble of searching for truth if no objective truth exists. If truth is merely whatever I think, at the end of the day – or the end of my life – I will have truth even though I've never expended any effort to find it. (Let's face it, as Christians we can be just as lazy as non-Christians when it comes to recognizing heresy and passing it off as merely a different way of saying – or a fresh way of perceiving – the same old truths).

The bane of fundamentalism is truth without grace. The bane of much postmodern evangelicalism (or post-evangelicalism, if you prefer) is grace without truth. This is tolerance, something much cheaper than grace, and which – unlike grace – doesn't require Christ to empower it.

Tolerance is the world's self-righteous substitute for grace. True grace recognizes truth and sin and deals with it in the most radical and painful way – Christ's redemption. Tolerance recognizes neither truth nor sin, and says "Everything's fine," negating or trivializing incarnation, redemption, and the need for regeneration. Christ came precisely because people are not fine without him.

Francis Schaeffer profoundly affected me and countless other young seeking minds in the '70s. We need to hear voices like his today. And we need to listen carefully as we talk with each other and especially with the young not only just in our culture, but also in our own homes and churches. We need to not simply hear the words they say, but also ask them, "What do you mean?" Then we need to say words back to them, words steeped in Scripture, and explain to them what we mean – which is hopefully what God means – by those revealed words. (Randy Alcorn, "Eternal Perspectives" Spring 2010, www.epm. org. Used by permission.)

Social and political liberals love to tout tolerance. In fact, they spout and tout tolerance as though it is their badge of honor.

It appears that there is no subject where they are more adamant about tolerance than the subject of homosexuality. Of course, they don't like us to use such an "abrasive" term – rather, they also tout the terminology of "being gay". At the outset I want to clarify that in my writing and speaking, I refuse to bow to the prevailing pressure to use their terminology to soften the more abrasive word homosexual. Why not? Because using the word "gay" is part of the calculated and planned strategy of the radical homosexual activists to change the perception of all Americans (all humans, actually) concerning their immoral practices. They not only want acceptance, they want dominance! They want us to comply with their terminology and bow to their demands. I refuse to comply. I do want to "speak the truth in love" as the Bible teaches, but true love is often tough love that does not compromise with evil. It does not comply with the enemies of truth by agreeing to their playing field or their distorted terminology. Therefore, the only time you will see the term "gay" in this book in reference to homosexuality, is when you read it in a quote from someone else.

The Danger of Compromise

Kenneth Beckman, retired professor at Boise Bible College, reminded us often, "When you compromise you become part of the problem you once sought to solve!" His resounding words ring true – and nowhere is it more evident than in the clash of worldviews with Biblical truth and morality on one side, crashing against evolutionism and homosexual immorality on the other side. Jesus was both the Master teacher and the Master Lover of all humanity, yet when He boldly confronted and exposed false teachers, He used some of the toughest language you will ever find in all literature. Consider these few verses from Matthew 23: *"Woe to you, scribes and Pharisees, hypocrites! For you travel land and sea to win one proselyte, and when he is won, you make him twice as much a son of hell as yourselves. Woe to you, blind guides, who say, 'Whoever swears by the temple, it is nothing; but whoever swears by the gold of the temple, he is obliged to perform it.' Fools and blind! For which is greater, the gold or the temple that sanctifies the gold?"* Matthew 23:15-17.

False Teachers

There are many, many religious leaders who are false teachers

promoting the homosexual agenda and proclaiming that people can come to Jesus "just as you are" – without change, without repentance. This is a bold, blatant lie! While their pagan or professed Christian colleagues are pompously parading their "Pride" in the streets, stripping off clothing, shocking innocent children with perverse practices, and glorying in their shame, the false teachers are lying to them by saying "I'm okay – you're okay. Jesus loves you just as you are. He made you that way and He doesn't require you to change your sexual orientation or practices." That kind of teaching is not love – it's lies! Yes, Jesus loves you just as you are, but He loves you too much to let you stay that way. The Gospel of Mark begins, *"The beginning of the gospel of Jesus Christ, the Son of God."* (Mark 1:1) and the first recorded words of Jesus in Mark's gospel are *"…"The time is fulfilled, and the kingdom of God is at hand. Repent, and believe in the gospel."* (Mark 1:15). **Repentance** = turn around (about face)! **It is essential to believing the gospel and accepting Jesus as Savior and Lord.**

What do you think Jesus will say to these false teachers? If you have been teaching this heresy, consider these verses: *"Therefore we make it our aim, whether present or absent, to be well pleasing to Him. For we must all appear before the judgment seat of Christ, that each one may receive the things done in the body, according to what he has done, whether good or bad. Knowing, therefore, the terror of the Lord, we persuade men; but we are well known to God, and I also trust are well known in your consciences.… Therefore, if anyone is in Christ, he is a new creation; old things have passed away; behold, all things have become new.… Now then, we are ambassadors for Christ, as though God were pleading through us: we implore you on Christ's behalf, be reconciled to God. For He made Him who knew no sin to be sin for us, that we might become the righteousness of God in Him."* 2 Corinthians 5:9-11, 17, 20-21. *"But the cowardly, unbelieving, abominable, murderers, sexually immoral, sorcerers, idolaters, and all liars shall have their part in the lake which burns* *with fire and brimstone, which is the second death."* Revelation 21:8. *I implore you with Peter's words: "Repent therefore and be converted, that your sins may be blotted out, so that times of refreshing may come from the presence of the Lord,"* Acts 3:19.

Secularization – The Spirit of the Age

What is the meaning of the word "secularization," and why do I call it the spirit of the age? Secularization is the mood, the mindset, the paradigm of those who have been brainwashed by evolutionism and Marxism. Briefly, secularization signifies the attitude not only that evolutionism is science, and Christianity (which they prefer to call religion) is faith - blind faith, but also that someone with a secular viewpoint is objective. Those of us who have faith in Jesus Christ as Lord are often considered prejudiced, biased, or ignorant. This is in spite of overwhelming objective proofs for the resurrection of Jesus and the historical and archeological accuracy of the Bible. Strangely, they are very open to people being "spiritual" – as long as that term means Wicca (witchcraft), Islam, Paganism, New Age Hinduism, or almost anything except Biblical Christianity. Why? Could it be because those religious (spiritual) systems come from the dark side (Satan), and do not require repentance and life change? I see a very strong bias – even prejudice and ignorance - concerning Biblical Christianity. Do you see it? Is that position objective? Who refuses to look at the evidence? Who is pre-judging? What do you think?

I've spent a lot of time around academia, especially in the past 12 to 15 years, and I notice the secularization mindset is especially strong on most campuses. So, if you go there expecting objectivity – don't be surprised if you are shocked by the level of bias you encounter!

> **"Man's way leads to a hopeless end.**
> **God's way leads to an endless hope!"**
> ~Anonymous

The Way of Salvation

Salvation is not easy believism. In our own strength, stamina, or self-righteousness it is impossible. But with God all things are possible. Salvation in Christ is a miracle of His grace. *"Therefore, if anyone is in Christ, he is a new creation; old things have passed away; behold, all things have become new."* 2 Corinthians 5:17

Charles Stanley says that God does not give us truth to consider – but to obey.

Salvation by Grace Through Faith

The Word of God makes it clear that God not only gives us truth to believe, but also to obey. Of course, if you do not believe Him, you will not obey Him. We are saved by grace through faith. *"But God, who is rich in mercy, because of His great love with which He loved us, even when we were dead in trespasses, made us alive together with Christ (by grace you have been saved), and raised us up together, and made us sit together in the heavenly places in Christ Jesus, that in the ages to come He might show the exceeding riches of His grace in His kindness toward us in Christ Jesus. For by grace you have been saved through faith, and that not of yourselves; it is the gift of God, not of works, lest anyone should boast. For we are His workmanship, created in Christ Jesus for good works, which God prepared beforehand that we should walk in them."* Ephesians 2:4-10; *"For we ourselves were also once foolish, disobedient, deceived, serving various lusts and pleasures, living in malice and envy, hateful and hating one another. But when the kindness and the love of God our Savior toward man appeared, not by works of righteousness which we have done, but according to His mercy He saved us, through the washing of regeneration and renewing of the Holy Spirit, whom He poured out on us abundantly through Jesus Christ our Savior, that having been justified by His grace we should become heirs according to the hope of eternal life."* Titus 3:3-7

What is Saving Faith?

Faith, (trust in Christ as the object of our faith) is essential to our salvation. Hebrews 11 is well known as the faith chapter. Please carefully note these verses near the beginning of the chapter: *"By faith we understand that the worlds were framed by the word of God, so that the things which are seen were not made of things which are visible . . . But without faith it is impossible to please Him, for he who comes to God must believe that He is, and that He is a rewarder of those who diligently seek Him."* Hebrews 11:3, 6

It is also important to note that true faith is obedient faith. **Professed faith that does not obey God is not trust, it is not saving faith.**

Please notice Jesus' own statement as to why He came into the world: *"Pilate therefore said to Him, 'Are You a king then?' Jesus answered, 'You say rightly that I am a king. For this cause I was born, and for this cause I have come into the world, that I should bear witness to the truth. Everyone who is of the truth hears My voice.'"* John 18:37. Did you also notice what he expects from us? Read that last sentence again! And what does he expect when we hear His voice? Consider what he bluntly told Nicodemus, the high-ranking Pharisee who came to Him by night. *"Jesus answered and said to him, 'Most assuredly, I say to you, unless one is born again, he cannot see the kingdom of God.' Nicodemus said to Him, 'How can a man be born when he is old? Can he enter a second time into his mother's womb and be born?' Jesus answered, 'Most assuredly, I say to you, unless one is born of water and the Spirit, he cannot enter the kingdom of God'. . . 'For God so loved the world that He gave His only begotten Son, that whoever believes in Him should not perish but have everlasting life. For God did not send His Son into the world to condemn the world, but that the world through Him might be saved. He who believes in Him is not condemned; but he who does not believe is condemned already, because he has not believed in the name of the only begotten Son of God. And this is the condemnation, that the light has come into the world, and men loved darkness rather than light, because their deeds were evil. For everyone practicing evil hates the light and does not come to the light, lest his deeds should be exposed.* **But he who does the truth comes to the light,** *that his deeds may be clearly seen, that they have been done in God."* John 3:3-5, 16-21. Did you catch that phrase in verse 21 where Jesus said, "he who does the truth"? Do you remember the quote from Charles Stanley? Here it is again: "God does not give us truth for consideration, He gives us truth for obedience." Charles did not just make up this idea, he got it from Jesus. The apostle John tells us in the last verse of John 3: **"Whoever believes in the Son** *has eternal life;* **whoever does not obey the Son** *shall not see life, but the wrath of God remains on him."* John 3:36 (ESV) Consider the apostle Paul's word to the Thessalonians: *"since it is a righteous thing with God to repay with tribulation those who trouble you, and to give you who are troubled rest with us when the Lord Jesus is revealed from heaven with His mighty angels,* **in flaming fire taking vengeance on those who do not know God, and on those who do not obey the gospel of our Lord Jesus Christ.** *These shall be punished with everlasting destruction from the presence of the Lord and from the glory of His power, when He comes, in that Day, to be glorified in His saints and to be admired among all those who believe, because our testimony among you was believed."* 2 Thessalonians 1:6-10

What is the Way of Salvation?

Jesus Himself is the Way of Salvation! He said, **"I am the Way, the Truth, and the Life. No one comes to the Father except through Me."** John 14:6. Wouldn't you be wise to hear Him? To believe Him? To obey Him? **"Then Peter said to them, 'Repent, and let every one of you be baptized in the name of Jesus Christ for the remission of sins; and you shall receive the gift of the Holy Spirit.'"** Acts 2:38

What is the Connection Between Repentance and Baptism?

The word "baptize" literally means immerse, and is translated "be immersed" in some versions of the Bible. **This makes perfect sense when we understand that in surrendering to the Lordship of Jesus Christ, a believer is proclaiming the gospel to the eyes of those who witness this monumental event, and at the same time declaring his or her willingness to die to sin and self, be buried, and rise again.** Consider Paul's question to believers in Rome: *"Or do you not know that as many of us as were baptized into Christ Jesus were baptized into His death? Therefore we were buried with Him through baptism into death, that just as Christ was raised from the dead by the glory of the Father, even so we also should walk in newness of life. For if we have been united together in the likeness of His death, certainly we also shall be in the likeness of His resurrection, knowing this, that our old man was crucified with Him, that the body of sin might be done away with, that we should no longer be slaves of sin. For he who has died has been freed from sin. Now if we died with Christ, we believe that we shall also live with Him, knowing that Christ, having been raised from the dead, dies no more. Death no longer has dominion over Him. For the death that He died, He died to sin once for all; but the life that He lives, He lives to God. Likewise you also, reckon yourselves to be dead indeed to sin, but alive to God in Christ Jesus our Lord."* Romans 6:3-11

Now consider his description of the essence of the gospel to the believers in Corinth: *"Moreover, brethren, I declare to you the gospel which I preached to you, which also you received and in which you stand, by which also you are saved, if you hold fast that word which I preached to you—unless you believed in vain. For I delivered to you first of all that which I also received: that Christ died for our sins according to the Scriptures, and that He was buried, and that He rose again the third day according to the Scriptures,"* 1 Corinthians 15:1-4. Now look again at Acts 2:38: *"Then Peter said to them, 'Repent, and let every one of you be baptized in the name of Jesus Christ for the remission of sins; and you shall receive the gift of the Holy Spirit.'"* What two commands are contained in this powerful verse? What two promises are there to be received? Now do you understand how the gospel is not only

43

a message to be received and believed, but also to be obeyed? **It is not in any way earning our salvation – it is submitting by faith to the Lordship of Jesus!** Do you also understand why there is no command to baptize babies in the New Testament Scriptures? Baptism is for believers, not babies! Can babies hear and understand the gospel? Can babies believe the gospel? Can babies obey the gospel? Can babies repent? Babies are already covered by the grace of God. *"But Jesus said, 'Let the little children come to Me, and do not forbid them; for of such is the kingdom of heaven.'"* Matthew 19:14

Jesus often told his followers to count the cost. What cost? Currently in America most people would not be threatened with bloodshed for believing, receiving, and obeying the gospel. That may change sooner than we think to become like fifty-five or fifty- six other nations where obeying the gospel could cost you your life. Americans now are likely to face some scorn and ridicule. So what? Consider these heavy words of Jesus: *"...Whoever desires to come after Me, let him deny himself, and take up his cross, and follow Me. For whoever desires to save his life will lose it, but whoever loses his life for My sake and the gospel's will save it. For what will it profit a man if he gains the whole world, and loses his own soul? Or what will a man give in exchange for his soul? For whoever is ashamed of Me and My words in this adulterous and sinful generation, of him the Son of Man also will be ashamed when He comes in the glory of His Father with the holy angels."* Mark 8:34- 38

Ananias warned Saul (later named Paul) what he would face, but also told him how God would powerfully use him to spread the gospel. Then he said: *"And now why are you waiting? Arise and be baptized, and wash away your sins, calling on the name of the Lord."* Isn't that a potent question for you to consider? Where is your faith? Where is your courage? *"For whatever is born of God overcomes the world. And this is the victory that has overcome the world—our faith. Who is he who overcomes the world, but he who believes that Jesus is the Son of God? This is He who came by water and blood—Jesus Christ; not only by water, but by water and blood. And it is the Spirit who bears witness, because the Spirit is truth. For there are three that bear witness in heaven: the Father, the Word, and the Holy Spirit; and these three are one. And there are three that bear witness on earth: the Spirit, the water, and the blood; and these three agree as one."* 1 John 5:4-8. Isn't it in baptism where all of these converge?

Amazing Faith and Commitment

I've read that once, when Patrick was baptizing a convert in Ireland, he jammed a spear with a Christian banner on it into the sand of the sea just before he dipped the man under the water. To his surprise, he noticed some red in the water as he raised the man up – and discovered that he had inadvertently jammed the spear through the man's foot. After apologizing to him sincerely, Patrick asked, "Why didn't you cry out?" The man replied, "I thought it was part of the commitment ceremony." What a clear perspective! Jesus shed His blood for you – are you willing to shed your blood for Him?

Paul wrote to the Colossians: *"I now rejoice in my sufferings for you, and fill up in my flesh what is lacking in the afflictions of Christ, for the sake of His body, which is the church,"* Colossians 1:24. Please realize that <u>when Jesus cried out, "It is finished!" there was nothing lacking in His sacrifice of blood for our salvation; however, the commitment to take that marvelous message of salvation to the ends of the earth has been costing the blood of the martyrs for nearly 2,000 years.</u> Consider this challenging article from the president of Voice of the Martyrs, November 2013:

> "Christians in Syria today are caught in the crossfire between a ruthless authoritarian regime and jihadist warriors who have swarmed to the region to fight what they consider a holy war to reclaim land. And the jihadists believe every bit of land they control is sacred Islamic territory.
>
> Many Christians have fled the violence, but many others have

remained in Syria for a variety of reasons. Some have stayed in the country because they have nowhere else to go, while others have stayed behind to answer a higher calling – a godly calling to reach the lost in Syria, even at the risk of their lives. Just last week, our staff met with one couple who are working to answer God's call in Syria. "Samer" and "Liena" are leaders in a boldly evangelical church that has continued to meet during the civil war; the church is growing rapidly even as the violence escalates.

Staying in Syria was not an easy decision for Samer and Liena. A church offered to sponsor their relocation to Europe and to provide housing, all living essentials and even private schooling for their two children. But after much prayer and fasting, they decided to continue their ministry at home.

'It was so hard living in a place where terrorists were coming from other countries,' Liena said. 'These men were saying, 'We will kill everyone who does not believe what we believe as Salafis and strict Muslims.' The couple knows, as do all Christians in Syria, that if their country falls into the hands of the radicals, Christians will be given three choices: convert to Islam, leave the country or die.

Samer and Liena threw themselves before God. They prayed, 'God, as Christians, what do you want us to do?'

'We were crying and praying,' Liena said. 'We fasted for many days. We put ourselves on the altar.' They prayed and fasted until they had made a decision. They would stay in Syria, no matter the cost.

One night as their neighborhood was heavily shelled by mortars, the family huddled together in the front room of their home. Liena pointed to the front door and said to her children, 'Look at this door. One day, God may allow someone from those terrorist people … to come in this door. They will have a big beard and very threatening faces, maybe they will have swords. They will put their swords on our necks, and you may see some blood. They will hurt us.

'We will have pain, but don't worry about this pain. We will close our eyes, and we will open them again in heaven, and we will be with Jesus, singing with the angels.

'Just tell these people, 'I forgive you, and Jesus loves you.' God did not call the family home to him that night. Instead, they continue to be lights for Christ in Syria. While they still have the option of leaving the country at any time, they feel strongly that God has them there for a purpose. One of those purposes is bringing attention to how Christians are suffering because of the war.

This month's newsletter focuses on the persecuted church in the historically rich nation of Syria, where brutal acts of war have drawn the attention of the world. The Voice of the Martyrs continues to stand with our brothers and sisters in Syria who boldly proclaim the love of Christ." (Material provided by The Voice of the Martyrs, PO Box 443, Bartlesville, OK 74003, 1-918-337-8015, www.persecution.com, thevoice@vom-usa.org. Used by permission.)

I believe "Samer" and "Liena" are taking seriously the commission the apostle Paul gave to Timothy, his son in the faith. Are you? Here is the commission: *"You therefore, my son, be strong in the grace that is in Christ Jesus. And the things that you have heard from me among many witnesses, commit these to faithful men who will be able to teach others also. You therefore must endure hardship as a good soldier of Jesus Christ. No one engaged in warfare entangles himself with the affairs of this life, that he may please him who enlisted him as a soldier."* 2 Timothy 2:1-4

Can you say as Paul did: *"I have been crucified with Christ; it is no longer I who live, but Christ lives in me; and the life which I now live in the flesh I live by faith in the Son of God, who loved me and gave Himself for me."* Galatians 2:20?

The Testimony of a Former Homosexual

Recently I heard the testimony of a former homosexual who spoke up during the open question and comment time following one of Ravi Zacharias' apologetic messages. He testified about how he repented and left behind the addiction to homosexual behavior, and stressed that although it was not easy, God gave him the victory. He no longer yields to the temptations and does not practice his sinful inclinations. I believe he said that it has been twenty years now that he is free from homosexual practices. He said that he was slandered and attacked not only by the secular crowd, but was also mocked and called a liar by professing Christians who told him he couldn't change – that it was impossible because he was "born that way." Like the blind man who was slandered and attacked by the religious leaders in Jesus' day, this man was slandered and attacked by "religious leaders" in our day. But like the blind man who said, "This I know – once I was blind, but now I can see", this ex-homosexual can say, "This I know – once I was a homosexual, but now I am free!"

If you are adamantly convinced that homosexuals can't change – please don't persecute those who have changed and are being changed by the power and grace of God. **"With God all things are possible!"** What are you going to do with the truth that homosexuals can change – and that many have by the power of God?

Dangerous Fundamentalists

It is my observation that atheists, humanists, and various types of left-wing liberals tend to lump Islamic fundamentalists and Christian fundamentalists together as dangerous fundamentalists. This is evidence that those who do so are either woefully ignorant of the facts or are intentionally distorting the facts to promote their own agenda, worldview, and prejudice. The basic fact is that Islam and Biblical Christianity are fundamentally different and polar opposites in many ways in spite of a few surface similarities. One of the most basic differences in the fundamental nature of these two faith systems was made crystal clear by a concise statement by former Attorney General John Ashcroft: **He said that Islam is a religion in which Allah rewards you for sending your son to die for him. Christianity is a faith in which God sent His Son to die for you.** Remember that fundamentals are the basics. With just a little study you can easily see that Islam and Christianity are only superficially similar – yet **basically very different!**

Another popular myth promoted by atheist (humanist) groups is that religion is the cause of most of the wars and bloodshed in all of human history. I want to point out three glaring flaws in this monumental lie: 1. They exclude their own religion of Humanism (a euphemism for atheism) from this broad sweeping incrimination. 2. They refuse to distinguish between the fundamental differences in religions. They do not acknowledge the possibility of true religion and false religion because they make the broad sweeping claim that all religions are false (theirs excluded, of course)! 3. They ignore the fact that the worst mass murderers in all of history – Stalin and Mao Tse-tung – were Marxist atheists. Together these two atheists orchestrated the deaths of over eighty million people. Hitler was a committed Darwinist who added a deadly mixture of occultism with Nietzsche's atheistic, anti-Christ philosophy. He was also responsible for the murder of millions of people, whom he considered sub-human scum. He and his Nazi henchmen were proud of speeding up the evolution processes by wiping out and eliminating the "culls' of humanity (and sub-humanity). **They gloried in their shame!**

Friend, if you are being tempted by atheism, please take a closer look at your philosophy. Isn't it leading you down a dead-end street of meaninglessness despair and destruction? I have been there. Atheism is a hopeless philosophy. Without God there is no design, no meaning, no purpose, and no hope. Dostoyevsky also accurately nailed down the fact that atheism has no morality. Although some atheists borrow their moral principles from Biblical theology, they actually have no logical basis for such morality. Dostoyevsky wrote that if there were no God, anything would be permissible. The truth of his statement is validated in Adolph Hitler. His near success in his massive effort to exterminate the Jews (and others he considered sub-human, enemies of the state, or worthless eaters) was under-girded by his philosophy – a potent mixture of atheistic Darwinism and Nietzscheism seasoned with deadly occultism. Like mixing drugs and alcohol – this powerful mixture of false philosophy and religion sparked the murder of millions and set off World War II. (Please see a more complete documentation of this in my book, *Ready to Give an Answer,* chapter 3, "Catastrophic Consequences of Darwinism".) Actually, Hitler was also a Marxist. Nazi means national socialist.

A Muslim man once told me that Hitler was a Christian. Whether he believed this lie because Hitler was born in Austria, which was once considered a Christian nation where Roman Catholicism was the dominant religion, believed it because Hitler was a master con-artist who manipulated both Catholic and Lutheran church leaders to coop-erate with his diabolical agenda, or if he merely told me this lie because it fit his own agenda, I do not know. **What I do know is that Adolf Hitler was not a Christian by Biblical standards, or by any stretch of an honest man's evaluation.** There is a plaque still on display at the Auschwitz death camp which says, *"I want to train up a generation of young people without conscience, impervious, relentless, cruel",* with Hitler's name on it as the author. Does that saying fit with Jesus' com-mands to turn the other cheek, forgive those who hurt you and to love your enemy? Ravi Zacharias candidly pointed out that it is never valid to portray any religion or philosophy by its distortions or aberrations. God does teach us in His Word to debate fairly and honestly accord-ing to truth and righteousness. *"For though we walk in the flesh, we are not waging war according to the flesh. For the weapons of our warfare are not of the flesh but have divine power to destroy strongholds. We destroy arguments and every lofty opinion raised against the knowledge of God, and take every thought captive to obey Christ,"* 2 Corinthians

10:3-5 (ESV). Those who build up straw men to knock down, then pound their chests and yell over their triumphs only parade their own foolish immaturity. Most of the blatant atheist/humanist books and blogs fit in this category – right along with a Muslim's portrayal of Hitler as a Christian. Twice God tells us in His Word, "The fool has said in his heart 'there is no God.'" See Psalm 14:1 and Psalm 53:1, then notice the rest of the verse: *"The fool says in his heart, "There is no God. They are corrupt, doing abominable iniquity; there is none who does good."*

It is true that there are some shameful blots on the pages of church history – and recent history. There are many who claimed the name of Christ who have sunk into gross corruption and committed atrocities. However, Ravi's concise, practical wisdom is **"Never judge a philosophy by its abuses."**

When Christians (or professing Christians) choose to yield to the flesh instead of the Spirit, they are capable of doing terrible evil and causing trouble and trauma for generations – even centuries. David, the prominent Psalmist of Israel, who was known as a man after God's own heart, became an adulterer, liar, and murderer when he yielded to the lust of the flesh. When Almighty God sent the prophet, Nathan, to tell David a captivating story and expose his corruption, David humbled himself and truly repented instead of proudly reacting in wrath by ordering Nathan to be executed or banished. In his humble repentance, powerfully expressed in Psalm 32 and 51, David once again became a man after God's own heart. Yet in spite of his deep repentance, David and his entire family (as well as the nation) suffered severe consequences for his sin.

When a Christian (or professing Christian) commits sin – even a terrible crime – what does it actually demonstrate? **It does not demonstrate that Christianity is false!** It does demonstrate that human nature is not basically good with a few superficial flaws (as humanism/atheism teaches). And it does demonstrate the truth and accuracy of God's Word concerning human nature. Consider this evaluation of human nature which the Holy Spirit inspired Paul to write to the Romans: *"What then? Are we better than they? Not at all. For we have previously charged both Jews and Greeks that they are all under sin. As it is written: 'There is none righteous, no, not one; There is none who understands; There is none who seeks after God. They have all turned aside; They have together become unprofitable; There is none who does good, no, not one.' 'Their throat is an open tomb; With their tongues they have practiced deceit'; 'The poison of asps is under their lips'; 'Whose mouth is full of cursing and bitterness.' 'Their feet are swift to shed blood; Destruction and misery are in their ways; And the way of peace they have not known.' 'There is no fear of God before their eyes.' Now we know that whatever the law says, it says to those who are under the law, that every mouth may be stopped, and all the world may become guilty before God. Therefore by the deeds of the law no flesh will be justified in His sight, for by the law is the knowledge of sin."* Romans 3:9-20. The law of God and the daily news reports confirm the depravity of man (often those their neighbors' thought were good), and our desperate need for the Savior. That is why Jesus came!

"God Sent Us a Saviour"

"If our greatest need had been information,
God would have sent us an educator.
If our greatest need had been technology,
God would have sent us a scientist.
If our greatest need had been money,
God would have sent us an economist.
If our greatest need had been pleasure,
God would have sent us an entertainer.
But our greatest need was forgiveness,
So God sent us a Saviour."

~ Roy Lessin

(©2013 DaySpring Cards. Used by permission,
all rights reserved. www.dayspring.com.)

All Spoiled and Blotted

Ravi Zacharias shares a story given to him by an elementary teacher. As I recall, it goes something like this:

He came to me with a quivering lip, and handed me his paper all spoiled and blotted. "I'm sorry, teacher, may I have another chance? I'm so sorry I spoiled this one!"

I smiled understandingly as I replied, "Here is a new one for you - do better now, my child."

I went to the throne with a trembling heart and handed God my day all spoiled and blotted. "I'm sorry, Father – may I have another chance? I am so sorry I've ruined this one."

His gracious eyes sparkled with love as He replied, "I forgive you. You have another chance – do better now, my child."

What Does God Want For You?

"For I know the thoughts that I think toward you, says the LORD, thoughts of peace and not of evil, to give you a future and a hope. Then you will call upon Me and go and pray to Me, and I will listen to you. And you will seek Me and find Me, when you search for Me with all your heart. . . 'Call to Me, and I will answer you, and show you great and mighty things, which you do not know.'" Jeremiah 29:11-13; 33:3

"Seek the LORD while He may be found, call upon Him while He is near. Let the wicked forsake his way, and the unrighteous man his thoughts; let him return to the LORD, and He will have mercy on him; and to our God, for He will abundantly pardon. 'For My thoughts are not your thoughts, nor are your ways My ways,' says the LORD. 'For as the heavens are higher than the earth, so are My ways higher than your ways, and My thoughts than your thoughts. For as the rain comes down, and the snow from heaven, and do not return there, but water the earth, and make it bring forth and bud, that it may give seed to the sower and bread to the eater, so shall My word be that goes forth from My mouth;

it shall not return to Me void, but it shall accomplish what I please, and it shall prosper in the thing for which I sent it." Isaiah 55:6-11

The Heart of the Problem is the Problem of the Heart!

Why was David a man after God's own heart? I believe the Word of God indicates it was because of his humility. Even after Samuel anointed him to be the next king of Israel while Saul was still on the throne, David humbly waited for God's timing to ascend to the throne. He still saw Saul as "God's anointed" and would not strike him down when he had opportunity after opportunity to do so – and in spite of the fact that Saul was trying to kill him. After David's terrible sins of adultery, murder and hypocrisy, God sent Nathan the prophet to expose him and confront him. If David were an arrogant man he would likely have said to Nathan, "How dare you accuse me?" He had the power to order Nathan to be exiled or executed – yet he did not react in arrogance and anger. David humbly confessed his sins and truly repented. The word of God teaches *"God resists the proud, but gives grace to the humble." "Humble yourselves in the sight of the Lord, and He will lift you up."* James 4:6, 8

The Deepest Rooted Sin

Pride is probably the deepest rooted sin in the human heart – and the hardest for us to detect in ourselves. Arrogance is like bad breath – the one who has it is the last one to notice that he stinks. A good test to tell if you have a proud heart is this – how do you deal with correction? If someone who cares for you points out a sin you need to repent of, do you react in anger or do you humbly consider the Word of God, repent, confess your sin, and ask forgiveness? *"If we confess our sins He is faithful and just to forgive us our sins, and to cleanse us from all unrighteousness."* 1 John 1:9. Are you humble enough to repent? Are you humble enough to thank the person who cared enough to confront you? Paul wrote to the Corinthians: *"Examine yourselves to see whether you are in the faith; test yourselves. Do you not realize that Christ Jesus is in you unless, of course, you fail the test?"* 2 Corinthians 13:5.

Here is another test of whether you have a humble spirit or an arrogant heart, whether you are truly converted – do you abhor (intensely hate) what is evil? Do you cling to what is good? *"Let love be without hypocrisy. Abhor what is evil. Cling to what is good. ... Do not be overcome by evil, but overcome evil with good."* Romans 12:9, 21

"I expect to pass through this world but once; any good things, therefore that I can do, or any kindness that I can show to any fellow creature, let me do it now; let me not defer or neglect it, For I shall not pass this way again."

~ Attributed to Etienne De Grellet (Public Domain)

The issue of a humble spirit before God is so crucial that the Holy Spirit inspired Paul to put it immediately after his strong exhortation to present our bodies as a living sacrifice to God, to refuse to be conformed to this world, and to be **transformed** by the renewing of our minds. Notice, *"I beseech you therefore, brethren, by the mercies of God, that you present your bodies a living sacrifice, holy, acceptable to God, which is your reasonable service. And do not be conformed to this world, but be transformed by the renewing of your mind, that you may prove what is that good and acceptable and perfect will of God. For I say, through the grace given to me, to everyone who is among you, not to think of himself more highly than he ought to think, but to think soberly, as God has dealt to each one a measure of faith."* Romans 12:1-3

It is also highly significant that he does not say that low self-esteem is the root cause of our bad behavior (nor does any other Biblical writer). Could it be that that teaching does not come from the Holy Spirit? **Self-control – not self-esteem is listed as fruit of the Spirit!**

Is This a Tangible Get-Rich-Quick Plan?

Here is an idea you may want to try; and because of the widespread and deeply rooted problem with mankind's over-inflated ego issues – it just might work. If you start an employment placement company, buy workers for what their actual skills are worth, and then sell them for what they think they are worth; it may be possible to quickly become a millionaire – then go on to become a billionaire! ☺

However, before you decide to start such a business, you may want to think it over very carefully about whom you will be working with and carefully ponder these verses: *"**The wicked in his pride persecutes the poor;** Let them be caught in the plots which they have devised. For the wicked boasts of his heart's desire; He blesses the greedy and renounces the LORD. **The wicked in his proud countenance does not seek God; God is in none of his thoughts**….His mouth is full of cursing and deceit and oppression; Under his tongue is trouble and iniquity. He sits in the lurking places of the villages; In the secret places he murders the innocent; His eyes are secretly fixed on the helpless."* Psalm 10:2-4, 7-8

Are All Religions Fundamentally the Same?

Ravi Zacharias has also clearly analyzed the false statement many people parrot that "all religions are fundamentally the same even though they have superficial differences". Ravi accurately says that the religions have a few superficial similarities even though they have huge fundamental differences. These differences include opposite teachings about our origin, destiny, purpose, meaning, morals and theology, as well as heaven, hell and salvation. Check it out! He's right!

The Word of God says: *"**Test all things; hold fast what is good. Abstain from every form of evil."** 1 Thessalonians 5:21-22, and "Beloved, do not believe every spirit, but test the spirits to see whether they are from God, for many false prophets have gone out into the world. By this you know the Spirit of God: every spirit that* *confesses that Jesus Christ has come in the flesh is from God, and every spirit that does not confess Jesus is not from God. This is the spirit of the antichrist,* which you heard was coming and now is in the world already. Little children, you are from God and have overcome them, *for He who is in you is greater than he who is in the world.* They are from the world; therefore they speak from the world, and the world listens to them. We are from God. Whoever knows God listens to us; whoever is not from God does not listen to us. **By this we know the Spirit of truth and the spirit of error. Beloved, let us love one another, for love is from God, and whoever loves has been born of God and knows God. Anyone who does not love does not know God, because God is love.** In this the love of God was made manifest among us, that God sent his only Son into the world, so that we might live through him. In this is love, not that we have loved God but that he loved us and sent his Son to be the propitiation for our sins. Beloved, if God so loved us, we also ought to love one another. No one has ever seen God; if we love one another, God abides in us and his love is perfected in us. By this we know that we abide in him and he in us, because he has given us of his Spirit. And we have seen and testify that the Father has sent his Son to be the Savior of the world. Whoever confesses that Jesus is the Son of God, God abides in him, and he in God. So we have come to know and to believe the love that God has for us. God is love, and whoever abides in love abides in God, and God abides in him. **By this is love perfected with us, so that we may have confidence for the day of judgment, because as he is so also are we in this world. There is no fear in love, but perfect love casts out fear.** For fear has to do with punishment, and whoever fears has not been perfected in love. We love because he first loved us. If anyone says, "I love God," and hates his brother, he is a liar; for he who does not love his brother whom he has seen cannot love God whom he has not seen. And this commandment we have from him: whoever loves God must also love his brother." 1 John 4:1-21 (ESV).

I choose to believe God! How about you?
Who do you choose to believe?'

True vs. False Religion

As a clear example of the difference between true and false religion, plus powerful testimony to the true meaning of love and joy in the midst of rejection and persecution, I want to share with you a summary of a VOM article by Todd Nettleton. (Published by Voice of the Martyrs, February 2013.) I encourage you to read the entire article.

Todd and a co-worker made a long, hot journey to visit Danmaya, a persecuted Christian in Nepal. Six years before, a friend has shared Christ with her – and she had received the good news of forgiveness in Jesus gladly. She was tired of trying to appease the millions of false gods of Hinduism, so was relieved to learn of the one God Who loved her so much He gave His only begotten Son to save her from sin and hell.

At first her husband thought that her faith in Jesus was only a passing phase, but when she was baptized, he knew she was serious, so he rejected her, turned her out in the street and married another woman. He felt she was dishonoring their high caste position. Her own parents also rejected her, but her spiritual family did not. The leader of the Christian congregation and his family opened their hearts and home to her and took her in as a member of their family.

It would seem perfectly normal to expect Danmaya to be a lonely, bitter, and destitute emotional wreck, but this is definitely not the case. She was tempted to hold bitterness in her heart toward her husband and parents, but chose to forgive by the example of Jesus, who prayed for those crucifying Him, "Father, forgive them for they know not what they do." Danmaya has discovered the key to the abundant life Jesus gives – and knows that the joy of the Lord is our strength! She couldn't keep from smiling – and was deeply grateful for the small gift Todd and his co-worker brought her.

"We drove almost two hours to meet Danmaya. But after hearing her story and seeing the radiant joy of the Lord on her face, I knew that I'd happily drive eight hours to spend one hour with such a Godly saint."

So, my friend, who were the intolerant ones in this story? Was it the fundamental Christians – or was it the fundamental Hindus? Will the left-wing propaganda change if liberals read multiple stories like this published by VOM and other mission organizations? **Most of the persecution of Christians is coming from Muslim nations or Marxist nations. Where are the news reports about this in the major media sources?**

Two Types of Fear

Unholy Fear = fearing what people think of you, what may happen to you, and everything else except God. *"The fear of man brings a snare, but whoever trusts in the Lord shall be safe."* Proverbs 29:25

Holy Fear = fearing God Himself, which gives us a holy boldness, spiritual knowledge, and godly wisdom. *"Fear not, for I am with you!"*

"And now, Israel, what does the Lord your God require of you, but to fear the Lord your God, to walk in all His ways and to love Him, to serve the Lord your God with all your heart and with all your soul, and to keep the commandments of the Lord and His statutes which I command you today for your good?" Deuteronomy 10:12-13

"Have I not commanded you? Be strong and of good courage; do not be afraid, nor be dismayed, for the Lord your God is with you wherever you go." Joshua 1:9

"And to man He said, 'Behold, the fear of the Lord, that is wisdom, and to depart from evil is understanding.'" Job 28:28

"The fear of the Lord is the beginning of knowledge, but fools despise wisdom and instruction." Proverbs 1:7

"Let us hear the conclusion of the whole matter: Fear God and keep His commandments, for this is man's all." Ecclesiastes 12:13

You won't often find wisdom in the halls of intellectualism, but you may find the epitome of human pride, arrogance, and foolishness. You will find both knowledge (science) and wisdom in a loving and surrendered relationship with our Father and Creator – Almighty God.

The Intolerant Tolerant Troop on Parade

Now to further illustrate the intolerance of the tolerant troop, I want to share with you a few brief articles from Christian news sources that are nearly completely ignored by the major media sources. Are they ignoring what is truly happening if it doesn't fit their leftist agenda?

"Want To Be Popular? Do Not Do This..."

"Want to be popular? Or want to avoid controversy?

Don't become a Christ-follower. If you take a clear stand for Jesus, or even for traditional biblical values, intimidation and criticism will likely come your way.

That seems evident in two stories in this issue of *Christian News Northwest*.

One is the news that New York quarterback Tim Tebow, widely known for his strong Christian faith, has backed out of a scheduled appearance at First Baptist Church in Dallas, Texas, later this spring.

That church has come under fire in the past year not only because of Pastor Robert Jeffress's unwavering view that the homosexual life-style is a sin, but also because of his belief that religions other than Christianity are heretical. Jeffress counters that his teachings are consistent with historic Christian beliefs and that his church is wrongly being characterized as hateful.

Like Jeffress himself, we were surprised and disappointed by Tebow's decision. It is obvious he was not prepared for the criticism he faced initially in accepting the church's invitation to speak. But we also feel some measure of sympathy for Tebow, because he simply may not have been aware of the extent of the controversy surrounding the Dallas church.

The other story, based here in Oregon but getting national attention, is Page 1 of this issue. Gresham business owners Aaron and Melissa Klein are being charged with discrimination because, as Christians, they didn't believe they should provide a wedding cake for a same-sex couple.

In this day and age, Christians such as Tebow, Jeffress or the Kleins are labeled as bigoted or hateful because of their Bible-based beliefs. This kind of attack isn't new – Christ-followers have been mischaracterized since the days of the early Church. But it sure is sad to see it happening in modern-day America." (John Fortmeyer, Publisher/ Editor, "Christian News Northwest", March 2013, Portland area. Used by permission.)

"Pastor Giglio No Longer Welcome On Inaugural Platform"

"In a sudden reversal with stunning implications for religious tolerance in America, aggressive and obviously influential homosexual activists pressured Pastor Louis Giglio to withdraw from offering the benediction at this month's presidential inauguration a few days after he accepted the invitation.

Giglio holds strong biblical views on homosexuality but has avoided the subject in his popular public ministry. A homosexual organization had to dig deep to find a 1990's sermon he preached which identified the practice as a sin based on standard Old and New Testament Scriptures. The group used the sermon to threaten a media-driven scandal, prompting Giglio to withdraw as quietly as possible.

News media started reporting the incident Thursday as simply a withdrawal on the pastor's part, but if he had done otherwise the presidential inauguration Committee would clearly have ousted him. As it was, the committee apologized for inviting him and promised to replace him with a "pro-gay pastor."

For discussion: This is a very public government rejection of a pastor simply for having once preached a Bible-based sermon on homosexuality. What could this precedent turn into long-term? We will have more information and analysis on this late-breaking development next week."

("The Times and the Scriptures," January 13, 2013. Used by permission of Norm Fox, owner and editor.)

"New – And Only – Black Senator Gets 'F' From NAACP"

"A black U.S. Senator has been a rarity lately. Neither party has had one for years, that is, until SC Gov. Nikki Haley (a rare Native American Republican woman!) appointed Rep. Tim Scott to replace the recently resigned Sen. Jim DeMint.

Sen. Scott is a pro-life, pro-traditional marriage Christian who favors repealing ObamaCare and cutting federal taxes, spending, and borrowing. That resume is probably enough to account for the fact that the National Association for the Advancement of Colored People is not celebrating this historic appointment of the first black Senator ever from South Carolina.

NAACP President Ben Jealous says Scott "opposes civil rights" because he favors a smaller government and that would work against "real issues of concern" to his organization's constituents. "We have some Republicans who believe in civil rights – unfortunately he is not one of them," Jealous said. The NAACP has given Scott an "F" rating because they rate "what's in people's hearts." The newly-seated Senator, asked for a response on a television interview, said that speaking as a black man raised by a low- income single mother, it is "ridiculous and baseless" to claim he is opposed to civil rights. "Mr. Jealous thinks bigger government means more freedom. I just totally disagree."

For discussion: Notice how moral/biblical issues such as some of those that distinguish Sen. Scott supersede other considerations that supposedly bind interest groups together. (Examples: a black organization that does not want to "advance" a black Senator, or women's organizations that will not support a pro-life woman.) Is that a good thing or not? How about a "gay rights" organization that opposes a homosexual's right to seek sexual orientation counseling? (See last week's lead article.) Does this just show that the most important defining classifications of people are the two described in Matt. 12:30?"

("The Times and the Scriptures," January 13, 2013. Used by permission of Norm Fox, owner and editor.)

"The Limits of 'Diversity'"

"Angela McCaskill is many things. She's the first black woman to earn a doctorate at Gallaudet University, a school for deaf people like herself. She's worked there for 23 years and is now the school's chief diversity officer.

Oh, and she's also suspended - technically, "on administrative leave"- because she's just a little too diverse for their taste.

McCaskill, you see, goes to church. And one day, after her pastor preached against same-sex marriage, she signed a petition at her church to let Maryland voters decide the issue. Seems she was under the impression that American citizens have the right to do such things.

Not any more, apparently. After a homosexual publication, the Washington Blade, got ahold of the signatures and posted them on line, a gay activist at the school noticed, complained to the higher-ups, and –bam! - McCaskill was suspended.

It may not last. She's got a lawyer, and the PR is terrible for Gallaudet, which - about 10 seconds after the story went national - announced it wants to work things out with her. Then again, it's been well over a month since then, so we'll see.

However this story turns out, it's clear what "diversity" really means to some people: Christians need not apply." (Originally appeared in the January/February 2013 issue of Focus on the Family's Citizen Magazine. Copyright © 2013 Focus on the Family. All rights reserved. International copyright secured. Used by permission.)

"California Bans Gay Change Therapy"

"In a stunning power grab orchestrated by homosexual activists, California has passed a law banning mental health professionals from offering minors any therapies meant to change sexual orientation.

The bill, passed by the state legislature and signed by Gov. Jerry Brown, was sponsored by state senator Ted Lieu, who is heterosexual. Gay activists have claimed for years that attempts to get kids to change sexual orientations are harmful and they have pushed for a law banning the practice.

"No one should stand idly by while children are being psychologically abused, and anyone who forces a child to try to change their sexual orientation must understand this is unacceptable," Lieu said.

But the law is extremely controversial because it allows the government to decide what types of therapies mental health professionals can use and, perhaps even more alarming, how parents raise their children.

The conservative Pacific Justice Institute said it will challenge the law in court.

"The privacy concerns are fairly significant," PJI staff attorney Matthew B. McReynolds told the Los Angeles Times. "In our view, it's an intrusion beyond what the government has done before."

Journalist Stephen Beale said liberals always seem to demand the freedom to choose for individuals – until the choice runs contrary to their worldview.

"Apparently, the possibility that a teenager may want to change his or her sexual orientation of their own accord – not due to the firm prodding of overbearing parents – never crossed their minds," Beale said." (AFA Journal, January 2013, p. 7. Used by permission.)

My Personal Experience with the Tolerant Troop

When will the "tolerant troop" become indignant and intolerant of gender and racial slurs like "male chauvinist pig," "homophobic bigot" and "old, fat white man"? When are they going to get outraged by death threats and obscene names called and sent to promoters of Proposition 8 for California and other Biblical marriage proponents? When are those who rail against hypocritical Christians going to rail against hypocritical tolerant troopers?

In August 1992 we moved to Gresham, Oregon, to help serve a local congregation there. In that city, as well as in neighboring Portland, I learned firsthand the intense bias of the homosexual activists against those who take a stand for Biblical morality and morals. I saw newspaper articles and cartoons blasting and mocking Lon Maybon – a conservative Christian man who dared take a public stand against the homosexual agenda. Since I had already experienced the slanted power of the press directed at me, I decided he couldn't be all bad if the liberal press hated him this much, so I went to see and hear him myself. What I experienced was not a wild-eyed radical as portrayed by left-wing media sources, but rather a soft spoken, Christian man with a backbone of steel. In his brief testimonial he described becoming increasingly disturbed by the encroaching and aggressive agenda of the homosexual activists while wondering, "Why doesn't someone do something to stop this?" He got the strong impression that God was calling him to do something to stop it, so he started a petition to block homosexual activists from promoting their agenda in the public schools. I doubt if he realized what a firestorm of protest, criticism, mocking, ridicule and slander he would unleash on himself by exercising his right and duty as a concerned American citizen. The longer I listened, the more I realized he was simply and straightforwardly articulating clear, Biblical morality in contrast with cultural corruption. The epitome of cultural clashes converge and culminate on the issues of sexuality and morality concerning contraception, abortion, sex education, and marriage. Lon Maybon touched a raw nerve and the liberal elite were determined to never let him forget it.

Some months later when I volunteered to help gather signatures, I experienced the most hate-filled glares I have ever seen. Was the tolerant troop tolerant of us – concerned American citizens? Hardly! Fortunately, there were many petition signers who commended us and urged us on – but not many were willing to commit to gathering petition signatures.

"I Have a Dream!"

September 15, 2013 was the 50th anniversary of Martin Luther King's famous speech. There has been great progress in racial relationships since that day – but much still needs to be accomplished. I also have a dream. **I dream of seeing another great awakening in America,** with genuine revival in our churches and millions of souls bowing to the Lord Jesus Christ and unreservedly giving their hearts to Him. **I earnestly desire spiritual awakening and pray daily for this. Will you join me?**

What can we do About It?

Again, I want to return to this question so that these news reports are not just an exercise in futility. So, what shall we do?

1. **Pray! Fervently pray! Every great awakening begins with prayer.** Remember – it's always darkest before the dawn, and "with God all things are possible". *"If My people who are called by My name will humble themselves, and pray and seek My face, and turn from their wicked ways, then I will hear from heaven, and will forgive their sin and heal their land."* 2 Chronicles 7:14

2. **We need to take seriously the Biblical responsibility of training our children** – and grandchildren if possible - in truth and righteousness. **Parents are the primary educators commissioned by Almighty God to instill a Biblical and Godly worldview in their children.** Bible teachers, Christian school teachers, youth leaders, and pastors/teachers are crucial and helpful as supplemental influences, but God commissioned parents with the task of training their children. Consider these Scriptures: *"Hear, O Israel: The Lord our God, the Lord is one! You shall love the Lord your God with all your heart, with all your soul, and with all your strength. And these words which I command you today shall be in your heart. You shall teach them diligently to your children, and shall talk of them when you sit in your house, when you walk by the way, when you lie down, and when you*

rise up. You shall bind them as a sign on your hand, and they shall be as frontlets between your eyes. You shall write them on the doorposts of your house and on your gates." Deuteronomy 6:4-9. Note: This same principle carries over to us as grafted in to Israel. Proverbs 22:6 says, *"Train up a child in the way he should go, And when he is old he will not depart from it."* Ephesians 5:33 says, *"Nevertheless let each one of you in particular so love his own wife as himself, and let the wife see that she respects her husband."* Note: The best way for children to learn how a man is to treat his wife and how a wife is to respect her husband is to see it modeled by their parents. Ephesians 6:1-4 says, *"Children, obey your parents in the Lord, for this is right. 'Honor your father and mother,' which is the first commandment with promise: 'that it may be well with you and you may live long on the earth.' And you, fathers, do not provoke your children to wrath, but bring them up in the training and admonition of the Lord."*

The best way for children to learn to develop the courage to stand for truth, righteousness, and against peer pressure is to see that courage of conviction modeled by their parents. Here is a great example from the April 2013 issue of Citizen Magazine, p. 9 in the section, "Overheard": "I'd rather have my kids see their dad stand up for what he believes in than to see him bow down because one person complained." Quoted from Aaron Klein, who is facing a state investigation because he and his wife wouldn't bake a wedding cake for a lesbian couple. Reported in Gresham, Oregon by KGW-TV, Feb. 2, 2013.

Speak up for truth and righteousness while we still can, in every way we can. Be strong! Be bold! Be active! Get involved! That is so much better than whimpering about what you should have done after it is too late.

"Do not boast about tomorrow, for you do not know what a day may bring forth." **Proverbs 27:1**

As an example of what we can do, here is a copy of a letter I wrote February 1, 2013 to the Leadership Team of the Boy Scouts:

"To the Leadership Team of Boy Scouts,

Please, please do not severely disappoint us by compromising with the homosexual agenda. I realize the homosexual activists are putting powerful pressure on you to comply with their agenda. We have admired you for standing strong for truth and righteousness – please don't abandon us now. I hope you stand against tyranny like Patrick Henry rather than compromising your integrity and committing treason like Benedict Arnold.

When facing overwhelming odds, Joshua needed reassurance. God spoke to him saying: *"Be strong and courageous, for you shall cause this people to inherit the land that I swore to their fathers to give them. Only be strong and very courageous, being careful to do according to all the law that Moses my servant commanded you. Do not turn from it to the right hand or to the left, that you may have good success wherever you go. This Book of the Law shall not depart from your mouth, but you shall meditate on it day and night, so that you may be careful to do according to all that is written in it. For then you will make your way prosperous, and then you will have good success. Have I not commanded you? Be strong and courageous. Do not be frightened, and do not be dismayed, for the Lord your God is with you wherever you go."* Joshua 1:6-9 (ESV)

Yours & His, Rick Deighton"

Unfortunately, the majority of Boy Scout leaders voted to allow practicing homosexuals to become scouts. However, this cowardly compromise did not satisfy the voracious appetite of the homosexual activists for power, control and total affirmation because the Boy Scout decision makers excluded homosexuals from leadership positions. (It was like trying to work out a compromise with a wild-eyed hungry tiger!)

Right Wing Radical?

Am I afraid that someone will call me a right wing radical? Not on your life! Why not?

1. Who is it who is being radical?

2. Satan is the father of lies – so why should I care if he inspires someone to call me radical? I would rather be right than wrong! Jesus Himself is seated at the right hand of the Father!

3. I would rather be considered a "right wing radical" than a fellow traveler with the left-wing liberals pretending to be loving.

Friend, if you have been traveling with the wrong crowd, please consider:

"Fools mock at sin, but among the upright there is favor. The heart knows its own bitterness, and a stranger does not share its joy. The house of the wicked will be overthrown, but the tent of the upright will flourish. There is a way that seems right to a man, but its end is the way of death. Even in laughter the heart may sorrow, and the end of mirth may be grief. The backslider in heart will be filled with his own ways, but a good man will be satisfied from above. The simple believes every word, but the prudent considers well his steps. A wise man fears and departs from evil, but a fool rages and is self-confident." Proverbs 14:9-16

"Do not be deceived: 'Evil company corrupts good habits.' Awake to righteousness, and do not sin; for some do not have the knowledge of God. I speak this to your shame." 1 Corinthians 15:33-34

It's time – past time to repent and come home to the Father. His heart aches for you and His arms are open wide. Now is the time! *"Do not boast about tomorrow, for you do not know what a day may bring forth."* Proverbs 27:1

The Holy Spirit commissions us to overcome evil with good. *"Let love be without hypocrisy. Abhor what is evil. Cling to what is good. . . Do not be overcome by evil, but overcome evil with good."* Romans 12:9, 21. Consider this powerful example from Breakpoint *(A Christian Perspective on Today's news and Culture):*

"The Sewer and the Dropbox"

"Overcome evil with good -- that was Chuck Colson's mantra.

And nowhere is it more applicable than in the fight against abortion, as one loving Korean pastor is proving.

The images and video broadcast around the world triggered shock and disgust: a team of Chinese firefighters sawed open a narrow sewage pipe and removed a screaming newborn baby. The tiny boy, whose only name was "59," after the number of his hospital incubator, miraculously survived after being flushed or dropped— we're still not sure—into a public sewer, where he became lodged.

Realizing what she says was a mistake, the baby's mother notified authorities, who rushed to the scene and dismantled the pipe piece by piece until the exhausted and frightened baby appeared. The young single mother says she meant to abort the baby when she found out she was pregnant—but couldn't afford the procedure.

Well, the good news is that Baby 59 is doing well and has since been taken home by his mother's family. And more good news is that the incident has brought China's abominable One Child Policy back to the fore of the world's attention, and highlighted the fact that—whatever the details of baby 59's case—countless infants are abandoned by their mothers in China every year because of this terrible, terrible law.

That's to say nothing of forced abortions and infanticide under the policy, another gruesome example of which emerged just days ago when a six-month pregnant woman died of hemorrhaging following a forced abortion.

But China isn't the only Asian country where being born alive is no guarantee of safe conduct. In South Korea, hundreds of infants are abandoned on the streets every year. The problem is so severe that one Korean pastor decided to take unprecedented action.

His story is the subject of an award-winning documentary by 22-year-old American film student, Brian Ivie.

Stirred by a report in the LA Times about Pastor Lee Jong-rak and his unique solution to infant abandonment, Ivie raised enough money to lead a team to Seoul, South Korea to capture this tiny but inspirational ministry.

Pastor Lee Jong-rak calls it his "Drop Box." The concept is simple. Instead of aborting or abandoning their infants, mothers who either can't keep or don't want their babies bring them to the wooden box affixed to Pastor Lee's house. They say goodbye, and shut the door. The box, which is equipped with lights and a heater, reads in Korean, "Please don't throw away unwanted or disabled babies, or babies of single mothers. Please bring them here instead."

When the box opens, a bell rings, and Pastor Lee, his wife, or a volunteer comes and takes the child inside. Since Pastor Lee installed the Drop Box in 2009, as many as 18 babies a month have arrived, and the same number of children currently live in his home, which doubles as an orphanage. He and his wife have even adopted ten of their own— the maximum number local authorities will allow.

Sometimes he speaks to the mothers face-to-face. One told him she intended to poison herself and her newborn before hearing about the Drop Box. Another simply left a note, which read:

"My baby! Mom is so sorry. I am so sorry to make this decision...I hope you meet great parents...I don't deserve to say a word. Mom loves you more than anything else. I leave you here because I don't know who your father is. I used to think about something bad, but I guess this box is safer for you...Please forgive me."

Brian Ivie's award-winning film of this incredible story is set for public release this fall. Come to BreakPoint.org to learn more about it.

The fight for life is more than just political. In so many ways, it's decided in the cultural imagination—and heroes like this provide the inspiration we need to replace cultures that spawned Kermit Gosnell, sewer pipes, child abandonment and forced abortions with a culture that looks more like the home of Pastor Lee Jong-rak.

That, my friends, is overcoming evil with good.

As John pointed out, Lee Jong-rak is a great example of what one person can do to overcome evil with good. Pastor Lee's ministry transcends politics and reaches to our imagination." ("Reprinted with permission of Prison Fellowship, P.O. Box 1550, Merrifield, VA 22116, www.colsoncenter.org.")

Ravi Zacharias says: "We never win a debate with hate." Jesus said: "You have heard that it was said, 'You shall love your neighbor and hate your enemy.' But I say to you, love your enemies, bless those who curse you, do good to those who hate you, and pray for those who spitefully use you and persecute you," Matthew 5:43-44. What if our enemies still hate us, yet accuse us of "hate crimes"? What shall we do then? Obey Jesus again!

The Proper Role of Family, Church, and State

Almighty God is the Creator and Master of family, church, and state. He designed each of these institutions carefully with a different role to play in an orderly society. Each is a minister (servant) for the Master – and answerable to Him.

The Bottom Line

"Yet in all these things we are more than conquerors through Him who loved us. For I am persuaded that neither death nor life, nor angels nor principalities nor powers, nor things present nor things to come, nor height nor depth, nor any other created thing, shall be able to separate us from the love of God which is in Christ Jesus our Lord." Romans 8:37-39

"For God has not given us a spirit of fear, but of power and of love and of a sound mind." 2 Timothy 1:7. Courage is not the absence of fear – it is the conquering of fear! You will not be inhibited by fear if you are inhabited by the Holy Spirit. **We are more than conquerors through Him who loved us.**

WE MUST BE COURTEOUS – BUT WE WILL NOT BE QUIET!

Potent Prayer

Lord, please fill me with Your Spirit and put me in the right place at the right time with the right words to honor You. Please give me the courage to confront and the grace to be courteous in the midst of our corrupted culture.

As you pray, remember that there are basically three kinds of people:

1. Those who are afraid.

2. Those who don't know enough to be afraid (the naïve).

3. Those who choose to trust God and believe His promises.

Supplement #1 for Chapter 2

I highly recommend these two articles by Tim Wildmon: *"White House, Media put American Lives at Risk by soft-pedaling Jihad"* (June 2013 afaJournal) and *"The Irony of Intolerance"* (September 2013 afaJournal). Contact information for afaJournal: P.O. Drawer 2440, Tupelo, MS 38803, www.afajournal.org. Also, the AFA has an excellent, pertinent article by Teddy James entitled "Faith and the Military - Can They Coexist?" in the AFA journal for January 2014.

Supplement #2 for Chapter 2

"A Letter to the International Pro-Family Movement

Posted on December 31, 2015 by Pastor Scott Lively. Used by permission.

I am Dr. Scott Lively, an attorney, pastor and President of Defend the Family International. For the past quarter century my ministry has been devoted to exposing and opposing the now-global homosexual movement, primarily in the United States, but with activity in more than thirty countries. I have been named public enemy number one by the world's largest homosexual organization, the Human Rights Campaign, labeled a "hate group" by the uber-leftist Southern Poverty Law Center, and targeted for personal destruction by the George Soros-funded Center For Constitutional Rights in a federal lawsuit (utilizing a team of fourteen lawyers), charging me with "Crimes Against Humanity" for preaching a reasoned, factual and non-violent message against homosexuality in Uganda.

I am in truth just a simple Christian missionary, running a one-man office with an annual budget of less than $120,000, but the enormously wealthy and powerful international homosexual network considers me one of its greatest threats. Why? Because I know nearly as much about their history, strategies and tactics as they do and my life's work has been to empower and equip pro-family activists around the world with those facts.

Importantly, I have personally experienced or been an eyewitness to every form of harassment, intimidation and sabotage that homosexualists employ to destroy anyone who dares to stand up to them. While I have known both male and female homosexuals who seemed like genuinely decent people despite being ensnared in sexual disorientation, I can confirm the warning of the Bible in Romans 1:24-32 that (in contrast) the Leaders and Activists of the LGBT movement are malicious deceivers and evil-doers, deliberately subverting civilized society and viciously attacking all opponents to advance their selfish and self-destructive interests.

I have paid a heavy price for the authority with which I speak, and I urge you to give credence to my testimony.

We must above all be honest with ourselves. With the Obergefell v Hodgess so-called "gay marriage" decision of the United States Supreme Court, the American pro-family movement has been set back dramatically – to a position equivalent to that of the pro-life movement in 1973. Indeed, Obergefell is rightly described by many as the Roe v Wade of the homosexual issue, which fact has profound implications for us all.

My ministry is one of only a dozen or so single-issue pro-family organizations in the United States who speak the truth about homosexuality boldly and unapologetically, most of which are similarly small and not well funded. With a couple of exceptions, the larger multi-issue Christian conservative groups are shackled by fear of the politically-correct media and are unwilling to base their arguments on the abnormality of homosexuality itself, acquiescing to many key homosexual demands such as civil unions and sexual orientation regulations, thereby severely undermining their moral authority.

One by one, all of the influential secular institutions of the United States have capitulated to a decades-long campaign of homosexual bullying and to such a degree that today even the once staunchly conservative US Chamber of Commerce has become a tool of "gay" social engineering.

The American public education system (from pre-school through graduate school), our social media giants, and the majority of our news and entertainment media are not just pro-homosexual, but militantly so.

Our government is in the hands of a man called "The First Gay President" by Newsweek magazine (which intended it as a compliment), who has made the global advancement of homosexuality such a priority of his administration that over $700 million has been devoted to it in just the past three years.

Only the Christian church (and Torah-faithful Jews) continue to stand against the homosexual agenda in America and most of the western world. However, subjected as it is to constant, aggressive pro- "gay" advocacy and suppression of pro-family dissent in the popular culture and key institutions, the church is weakening, especially among its most vulnerable members, the youth.

That is the unfortunate reality not just in the United States, but the UK, Canada, the EU, and much of the rest of the western world.

Yet, though our situation is dire, even in the United States there remains work that can be done to reverse the current trend for those with long-term vision. And if we adopt a global perspective, and are willing to build international cooperation with morally-conservative countries (who still represent the vast majority of the world's population), there is realistic cause for optimism.

In my view as a veteran Christian missionary to the international pro-family movement there are three things we must do.

• Inoculate the Church Against "Gay Theology"

• Repeal or Amend All Sexual Orientation Regulations and Restore the Right to Discriminate Against Homosexual Conduct

• Persuade Family-Friendly Nations to Ban Homosexual Propaganda to Children

I urge every pro-family advocate across the world to personally adopt the three simple goals outlined in this letter and to work toward their implementation. I further offer my services as a consultant, lecturer and/or strategist to assist pro-family advocacy groups around the world to achieve these goals.

Lastly, let us all pray that 2016 will be the year when the LGBT global campaign to homosexualize the world will finally be turned back.

Your Ally in the Cause of Truth,
Dr. Scott Lively"

Note: What you have just read is an abbreviation of the full article. To read the full article please use this contact information: www.defendthefamily.com, www.scottlively.net. You just may find much more interesting information

Questions for Chapter 2: How Truly Tolerant is the Tolerant Troop?

1. What is the difference between the dictionary definition of "tolerance" and the current post-modern usage of the word?

2. Is the new meaning of this word accurate or twisted? Explain your answer.

3. Sometimes in friendships or in family relationships it is necessary to compromise our opinions and preferences for the sake of peace; however, what happens if we compromise on matters of truth and righteousness?

4. The Biblical teaching about salvation is not easy believism. What very important truth is often deleted and avoided in many (if not most) churches attempting to be seeker sensitive (or seeker driven)?

5. If homosexuals can't change, how do you explain former homosexuals who have changed?

6. Who are the dangerous fundamentalists?

7. What is the heart of the problem?

8. Are all religions fundamentally the same? Explain your answer.

9. Can you name two examples of intolerance among those who profess to promote tolerance?

10. How can we promote positive change?

CHAPTER 3:

Phony Matrimony vs. Merry Marriage

(Con-artists are still Selling Genuine Imitations)

To begin this chapter, I want to share with you two brief articles from our February 2013 prayer letter for Overseas Outreach:

The Sanctity of Marriage and Life

Dear Friends & Prayer Partners,

The sanctity of marriage and the sanctity of life are intricately interwoven and founded in Scripture all the way back to Genesis, the Book of Beginnings. It was God Himself who said: *"'Let Us make man in Our image, according to Our likeness; let them have dominion over the fish of the sea, over the birds of the air, and over the cattle, over all the earth and over every creeping thing that creeps on the earth.' So God created man in His own image; in the image of God He created him; male and female He created them. Then God blessed them, and God said to them, 'Be fruitful and multiply; fill the earth and subdue it; have dominion over the fish of the sea, over the birds of the air, and over every living thing that moves on the earth.'"* Genesis 1:26-28

Note that God Himself created them male and female. He is the Originator of marriage, and He told them to reproduce (sanctity of marriage and family). Hebrews 13:4 reads, *"Let marriage be held in honor among all, and let the marriage bed be undefiled, for God will judge the sexually immoral and adulterous."* (ESV).

By inspiration of the Holy Spirit the apostle Paul labeled "forbidding to marry" as a "doctrine of demons" (1 Timothy 4:1-3). Why? Because demons know that forced celibacy backfires into misuse and perversions of sexual desire. (It is now costing the Roman Catholic Church not only much shame and scoffing, but also millions of dollars). Demons promote perversions, inflame passions and invite promiscuity, whereas God promotes the commitment of one man and one woman to each other for life in monogamous marriage. The children born into such a loving committed union are far more likely to grow up to be happy, healthy, helpful and holy than those from broken homes. Joe Garman, founder of American Rehabilitation Ministries, told me that prisoners send out millions of Mother's Day cards, but rarely request Father's Day cards. You don't suppose that the absence of a loving father's guidance contributed to their criminal activity, do you? What a shocking thought for those with a "politically correct" mindset. Our government not only undermines marriage with its welfare rules, but our courts have even sanctioned the production of pornography and sadistically violent video games as "freedom of speech" under our Constitution. Our founding fathers would be horrified at such perversions – but demons rejoice. By the way, you don't suppose that the "doctrine of demons" has any influence in Hollywood, do you?

This month we celebrate Valentine's Day, which can also be easily distorted and perverted, but let's truly celebrate the joy and wonder of romantic love in committed marriages. Valentine was a courageous pastor and Christian leader in the third century, who honored the sanctity of matrimony as God's institution by continuing to perform wedding ceremonies for young couples even after Caesar's decree "forbidding to marry" was announced. Caesar wanted more men to enlist in his military and feared that marriage would be a deterrent to his conquests. Valentine paid for his commitment to marriage with his life and is honored as a Christian martyr. Are you committed to truth and courageous enough to speak up for Biblical marriage in a world gone mad?

To honor the sanctity of marriage I want to share with you copies of the letters Della and I wrote to each other and displayed at our 50th Wedding Anniversary celebration. We hope and pray that many of you also grow in your love and commitment to your spouse through the years and that your relationship with God grows "sweeter as the years go by".

Dear Rick,

- *I love the fact that you are sold out – heart and soul – to God.*

- *I love your diligence and love for the study of God's Word. Your Bible knowledge amazes and inspires me.*

- *I love your tenderness with me when I'm hurting or not feeling well.*

- *I love your sense of humor.*

- *I appreciate your love for our children and grandchildren.*

- *I love to see your eyes light up and your big smile when Trinity does something cute.*

- *I love to see you dance around the house when music fills the air.*

- *I love you for being quick to forgive me when I've been irritable and "hard to live with".*

- *I love you because I know I can trust you to be faithful to me – even when you are far away in Ukraine or somewhere else.*

- *I love you for being persistent in business, even when there is one frustrating thing after another to deal with.*

- *I love you for your honesty and integrity in business, in ministry, in personal relationships.*

- *When you've been misunderstood and your ministry has been undermined, you have simply committed it to God and continued to serve Him. I love you for that humble spirit, Rick.*

Some of our friends will also remember the song "Peggy Sue" that was popular when we were teenagers, but may never have thought of the fact that the name Della Lu fits just as well in the poetic rhythm of the song. Here is my altered version of a few words from the song:

I love you, Della Lu, with a love so rare and true – Oh Della – Oh Della Lu (ooo – ooo – ooo - ooo)!

Why do I love you, Della Lu? Here are seven reasons – isn't seven the perfect number?

1. *I love you because your beautiful smile (which says, "I love you") lights up my life like a glorious sun break on a winter day in western Oregon – and it sets my heart to fluttering all over again.*

2. *I love you because your integrity is deep and strong (as when you quit a very good paying job rather than to buckle under the pressure to lie for the company).*

3. *I love you for your deep loyalty to your commitments, your friends, and to me.*

4. *I love you for your devotion to Christ, to His church, to His mission, and to your family.*

5. *I love you for being a frugal, diligent, hard-working, productive wife – as described in Proverbs 31.*

6. *I love you for your careful attention to details – which makes you a superb bookkeeper and treasurer for our business, our mission, and our personal finances.*

7. *I love you for your service as my volunteer secretary who turns my hand-written scribbles into legible letters, emails, articles, reports, booklets and books. Back in our Bible College days at BBC, Kenny Beckman once wrote on my report: "A – thanks to a devoted wife". Some glorious Day I may hear from our Lord, 'Well done, good and faithful servant – thanks to a devoted wife!'*

How to Handle Conflict

Because of our innate differences, any two people (or more) who live together will sometimes irritate each other, and because we all inherit a selfish nature, sometimes our wills will clash. There will be conflict. **The key to having good relationships is learning how to handle conflict.** Some conflicts will be mild; some may be explosive. Since not one of us is always right, there are four phrases that make a marriage work:

I was wrong

I am sorry

Please forgive me

I love you

These four phrases are based on the Biblical principles of love, acceptance, and forgiveness. In fact, these same principles and phrases build beautiful relationships – not only in marriage but also in family and friendships. However, don't try using these phrases as a gimmick. No one loves and appreciates a hypocritical con-artist. Honesty is the best policy!

Distorted Diversity Produces Profane Perversity

Should we be so open-minded that we cave in to the "politically correct" crowd who wants us to believe that so-called "gay marriage" is the wave of the future (and the present), and that we should accept their warped mantra that the loving thing to do is accept it? Those who oppose "gay marriage" (according to their agenda) are guilty of "hate speech." One of Ronald Reagan's witty sayings is especially appropriate here: *"Some people are so open-minded their brains fall out!"*

Has it ever occurred to you how much our corrupt culture has distorted diversity because of the convoluted concepts of 'political correctness'? Almighty God created true diversity when He Himself created human beings male and female and He Himself ordained the marriage of one man to one woman. Why?

1. **It takes the unique characteristics of both male and female to reflect the image of God!** Consider the record: "Then God said, 'Let Us make man in Our image, according to Our likeness; let them have dominion over the fish of the sea, over the birds of the air, and over the cattle, over all the earth and over every creeping thing that creeps on the earth.' **So God created man in His own image; in the image of God He created him; male and female He created them.**" Genesis 1:26-27

Notice that God by His very nature is unity in diversity! He said, "Let **Us** make man in **Our** image"! The concept of one God existing as unity in plurality from the very beginning is expressed here in the first chapter of Genesis. Colossians chapter one tells us that Jesus created all things, and Colossians 2:9 tells us, "in Him dwells all the fullness of the Godhead bodily". Genesis 1:1 says, 'In the beginning God created the heavens and the earth." Genesis 1:2 says "And the Spirit of God was hovering over the face of the waters." The concept of one Almighty God with the plurality of His nature is to be reflected in **man** (human beings) existing as male and female. Although God is **always** referred to in Scripture as He, some of His characteristics are best reflected by the female side of humanity. For example, God's love is portrayed as even greater than that of a nursing mother for her own child. Therefore God chose to create humans as male and female to reflect His image. However, men learn how to be the courageous and bold protector of their children (tough) balanced with the playful moments holding them or tousling their hair (tender) by being imitators of God.

2. **He ordained marriage and told Adam and Eve to be fruitful and multiply. It was God Himself who created humans as sexual beings able to reproduce children**. God ordained marriage both for companionship and for the union of a man with his wife to produce godly offspring! God inspired Malachi to expose the treachery of profaning the marriage covenant. *"Have we not all one Father? Has not one God created us? Why do we deal treacherously with one another by profaning the covenant of the fathers? ... Yet you say, 'For what reason?' Because the Lord has been witness between you and the wife of your youth, with whom you have dealt treacherously; yet she is your companion and your wife by covenant. But did He not make them one, having a remnant of the Spirit? And why one?* **He seeks godly offspring. Therefore take heed to your spirit, and let none deal treacherously with the wife of his youth."** Malachi 2:10, 14-15. *"Husbands, likewise, dwell with them with understanding, giving honor to the wife, as to the weaker vessel, and as being heirs together of the grace of life, that your prayers may not be hindered."* 1 Peter 3:7

The so-called 'marriage' of a man with a man or a woman with a woman is perversity – not diversity. It distorts the purposes of marriage and profanes "the Lord's holy institution which He loves" (Malachi 2:11). Basic Biblical theology and basic human anatomy expose the basic human depravity of those distorting diversity by promoting "same sex marriage". Homosexuality is still called an abomination and perversion in God's Holy Word. (See Leviticus 18:22 and 1 Corinthians 6:9-11.) **Politically correct concepts convolute and**

corrupt God's holy institution of marriage and every other subject they touch. Remember, **"Beware lest anyone cheat you through
philosophy and empty deceit, according to the tradition of men,
according to the basic principles of the world, and not according to
Christ. For in Him dwells all the fullness of the Godhead bodily;"**
Colossians 2:8-9

Now I want to share an excellent article by Bob Russell, which Victor
Knowles printed for Viewpoint June/July 2012 of the Knowlesletter:

"President Obama vs. Biblical Truth on the Issue of Gay Marriage"

"President Barack Obama came out in favor of same sex marriage
last week, the first President of the United States to do so. As expected,
liberals in the media are praising the President's stand as 'courageous'
and 'aligning himself with the entire world in standing for civil rights.'

An increasing number of liberal church leaders are also endorsing
the gay life style; even ordaining homosexual ministers and performing gay marriages. Liberal churches rationalize their stance by pointing out that while the Old Testament condemns same-sex relationships, Jesus said nothing about it, so it must be okay.

Granted, there is no recorded statement from Jesus on the subject
of homosexuality. However, we have no direct quote from Jesus about
slavery or rape either. So, obviously, the absence of a statement from
Jesus doesn't qualify as an endorsement.

Furthermore, it isn't just the recorded words of Jesus that followers of Christ consider to be God's Word. The entire New Testament
is regarded as God-breathed (2 Timothy 3:16) and the standard of
absolute truth. Right and wrong are not determined for us by personal
emotion, majority opinion, current trends, or influential experts, but
the Bible. Jesus prayed, 'Sanctify them in the truth, your word is truth.'

The New Testament book of Romans states: 'Because of this, God
gave them over to shameful lusts. Even their women exchanged
natural relations for unnatural ones. In the same way the men also

abandoned natural relations with women and were inflamed with lust for one another. Men committed indecent acts with other men, and received in themselves the due penalty for their perversion.' (Romans 1:26-27)

Clearly, both the Old and New Testaments forbid same sex relationships. Although each individual has innate strengths and weaknesses and we are vulnerable to different temptations, none of us is given a license to yield to our base, carnal desires. We're told, 'deny self' and, 'abstain from the evil desires that war against your soul.' To endorse gay marriage is to disregard the plain teaching of Scripture.

The question is not whether the Bible condones same sex marriage – it clearly does not. The question is whether Christian leaders will be courageous enough to take a Biblical stand and accept the inevitable persecution that will follow or will we just say what itching ears want to hear? Will we stand for God's truth or embrace the spirit of the age?

Folks, this is not a political issue. It's a spiritual issue that goes to the very core of our belief system. God ordained marriage in the Garden of Eden as sacred. If believers don't have the courage to stand up for marriage, then we are not worthy to be called followers of Christ.

Kudos to the Roman Catholic Church. The pope and many local bishops are speaking out fearlessly on this issue. It's time for evangelical leaders to stand up and be counted as well. I've observed that many Bible-believing preachers are weary of the battle and are growing strangely silent on the subject. They're apprehensive of being accused of being homophobic and lacking compassion. Many are dodging the issue in hopes their church will not be branded with a negative image in the community.

Martin Luther once said, **'If I be valiant all along the battle line except at the point where Satan presses his attack, I am not valiant for Christ.'** Satan is directly attacking the sanctity of life, the sacredness of marriage and religious liberties. This is no time for us to grow weary in doing good. **Now more than ever we need Christian leaders**

87

to be strong and courageous. Admittedly, you're going to be labeled homophobic and intolerant. The bullies in the gay and lesbian community will hurl insults at your church, accuse you of hate speech and being out of step with where the culture is heading.

I beg you to remember that Jesus said, 'If you're ashamed of me AND MY WORDS then I will be ashamed of you when you stand before my Father who is in heaven.' And 'Blessed are you when people insult you, persecute you and falsely say all kinds of evil against you because of me. Rejoice and be glad, because great is your reward in heaven.' (Matthew 5:11-12)" (Bob Russell, "The Knowlesletter", June/July 2012, "Viewpoint." Used by permission.)

As backup information to the articles shared so far in this chapter, I now quote from the February 27, 2011 issue of *The Times and the Scriptures Weekly Bulletin:*

"Obama Declares Marriage Defense Unconstitutional"

He's Decided Homosexuality is "Immutable"

"In a stunning move that must have the Supreme Court wondering whether it still has any role in government, President Obama Wednesday declared the Defense of Marriage Act (DOMA) unconstitutional and instructed the Justice Department to stop defending it in court. Attorney General Eric Holder, only too happy to comply, has already notified courts that the federal government is pulling out of all related cases, even those already in progress.

Holder announced, 'The president and I have concluded that Section 3 of DOMA is not constitutional,' and that 'sexual orientation is an immutable characteristic.' That notion, of course, is disputed by professionals who can find no genetic cause for the behavior, and certainly by former homosexuals, but it was foundational to this executive declaration of unconstitutionality.

The executive proclamation was a step toward fulfilling predictions that the repeal of 'Don't Ask Don't Tell' by the lame duck

Congress would hasten the onset of nation-wide 'gay marriage.' (Review 1-2-11 *Bulletin*) Holder's statement cited that repeal as evidence that 'the legal landscape has changed' since 1996 when DOMA was passed and signed by President Clinton.

Some experts see a silver lining in the presidential power grab. Congress can intervene in defending duly-passed laws, and the House might step in to defend DOMA despite the Obama-Holder surrender. Heritage Foundation's Chuck Donovan says the law may now get better defense than the 'half-hearted farce of a representation [by] the Obama Justice Department.' Christian legal organizations might now be welcome to help defend DOMA. Matt Staver of Liberty Counsel says, 'This law has been attacked before and upheld as constitutional.'" ("The Times and the Scriptures", Weekly Bulletin for February 27, 2011. Used by permission.)

Answers Magazine for October-December 2012 carried this brief article:

"Homosexual Marriage – Golden Rule for Marriage?"

"ACCORDING TO PRESIDENT OBAMA, his view of marriage has "evolved" since his election. He now supports homosexual marriage. While this may not surprise those who have followed his metamorphosis his reasoning may:

[Michelle and I are] both practicing Christians. . . .But, you know, when we think about our faith, the thing at root that we think about is not only Christ sacrificing himself on our behalf, but it's also the Golden Rule, you know? Treat others the way you would want to be treated.

In 2008, President Obama said, 'God's in the mix' for defining marriage, which at that time he asserted was strictly between a man and a woman. But he now says the Golden Rule (the concept Christ taught in Matthew 7:12) compels him to endorse so-called gay marriage.

However, that sort of thinking twists Scripture. When Jesus gave the Golden Rule, He said it sums up the Old Testament's teachings. That would include both the creation of marriage between a man and a woman in Genesis 2:18-25 (which Jesus affirmed in Mark 10) and God's decree against homosexual behavior in Leviticus 18:22.

When given a chance to weigh in on the issue, American voters continue to affirm a position consistent with God's Word. In all 32 states where same-sex marriage has been put to the voters, they have rejected it. Most recently, North Carolina voted 60%-40% to affirm biblical marriage in the state constitution. Every state that has allowed same-sex marriage has ignored voters and gone through the courts or legislatures.

While treating others as we want to be treated is at the foundation of Christianity, it does not allow us to rewrite Scripture. Jesus guaranteed that Scripture would never change (Matthew 24:35) – even if politicians' views do." ("Answers Magazine", October-December 2012, Used by permission.)

An Open Letter to My "Progressive" Friends (Do I become your Enemy because I tell you the Truth?)

Rick Deighton

Does the fact that I believe the Word of God is true make me outdated and bigoted? I sincerely believe that God's command to me to "be content with such things as you have", applies not only to my finances but also to my own body and its separate parts. I remember that the Word of God distinctly tells us that it was God Himself Who created human beings as male and female – equal, but separate and distinct. Their equality is demonstrated in the fact that He gave **them** dominion over the earth, the sea and the creatures in earth's domain. See Genesis 1:26-28.

Am I outdated because I believe that a man should walk, talk and act like a man? That he should be the strong leader of his family and be their primary provider and bold protector? Also that a woman should look, walk, talk and act like a woman? As a matter of fact, God has some very clear instructions about these matters in His Word!

Who Has the Right to Determine what is Evil?

Evil is the violation of our Creator's purpose. This is why Dostoyevsky's comment is so pertinent and powerful: "If there were no God, anything would be permissible." This is also why secular humanists have no objective standard for morality. All they can do is shout and parade their own biased opinions.

The Ultimate Confusion

During the late 1960's, another Christian leader and I were meeting together with a student from Northwest Christian College to pray for the unity of the body of Christ. One day he shared with us a deep burden on his heart – cross dressing. Sometimes when all alone he would dress in women's clothing. He was ashamed of himself for doing this and only came to bare his soul before us because he felt we would continue to accept him and pray with him for victory over this temptation to pretend to be a woman in spite of the fact that God created him to be a man. We did.

I recognize that there is such a condition as gender confusion - and it has gotten much worse than it was when I was a kid because of the massive homosexual advertising campaign passionately promoted by Hollywood. In fact, it appears that homosexuals and Hollywood are now bonded with superglue! All kids are confused about some things, but with godly training, experience and maturity, most of them outgrow even sexual identity confusion. Little girls who wanted to act like tomboys and little boys who liked dolls usually grew up just fine before the campaign to solidify their confusion, warp their maturing process, and push them like pawns for promoting homosexual agendas. The

Bible says, "foolishness is bound up in the heart of a child", but warped wisdom and twisted tenderness teaches us not to try to change their confusion with the cold hard facts. A male is a male down to every last cell in his body! A female is a female down to every last cell in her body. (This is a scientifically verifiable fact. Check it out if you doubt - and be sure to check reliable sources.) No amount of twisted tenderness or sharp **scalpels performing "sex change surgeries" will ever change the fact of who God created you to be.**

God, our Father, designed male and female for sacred, sanctified sexuality. Satan seeks to substitute selfish, sordid sexuality with its cheap thrills to steal, kill and destroy our joy and pervert God's design.

Sexual Molestation Causes Confusion and Leaves Deep Scars!

There is very strong evidence that many, if not most, gender confused individuals were sexually molested as children. If you are one of those individuals, my heart aches for you. You very likely have deep fear and anger issues to work through. However, remember that you are responsible for your actions and attitudes now – as an adult. **You are not guilty for the actions of the pedophile who molested you, but if you who were molested follow in the same wicked path and become a molester, you are guilty!** God can and will break your bondage and set you free. He will forgive you and transform your life by the blood of Jesus and the power of the Holy Spirit if you surrender your will to Him and accept His forgiveness, His grace, His power. Then He can use you as His tool to help rescue others from their bondage. *"'Come now, and let us reason together,' Says the Lord, 'Though your sins are like scarlet, they shall be as white as snow; though they are red like crimson, they shall be as wool.'" Isaiah 1:18. "And you will seek Me and find Me, when you search for Me with all your heart." Jeremiah 29:13. Can you pray as Isaiah did? "Yes, in the way of Your judgments, O Lord, we have waited for You; the desire of our soul is for Your name* *and for the remembrance of You. **With my soul I have desired You in the night, yes, by my spirit within me I will seek You early; for when Your judgments are in the earth, the inhabitants of the world will learn righteousness.***" Isaiah 26:8-9

Self-Centered Pride is the Core of Rebellion Against God

I remember in my teens going through a "rebel without a cause" stage. The basic problem was that I simply didn't want **anyone** – not even **God** – telling me what to do (or not to do)! I needed to repent, for the Word of God teaches that rebellion is as the sin of witchcraft (1 Samuel 15:23). Are you a grown man or woman (or a teen) still nursing and coddling an adolescent attitude of rebellion? Pride and self-centeredness are at the core of all sinful rebellion. "I want what I want when I want it and how I want it," is the manifestation of that sinful attitude. I implore you to wake up to reality! Your family and friends, the whole world, and God Himself, do not revolve around you! **Jesus loves you more than you can possibly realize!** Yes, with all your hang-ups, confusion and rebellion, He still loves you. **Sometimes His love is tough love. He is not an enabler. He loves you too much to leave you as you are.** You may fight and struggle and reject Him with His austere commands, but **I hope you at least come to recognize and realize that all of His commands are for our own good – whether we like them or not.** If you were taking care of a two-year-old child who wants to play with a sharp knife – would you let him have it? If he gets upset, screams, and throws a tantrum, would you give it to him? I hope not! Why not? Because you care for him. You know better than he does what is good for him and what will harm him.

Are you Contentious?

Consider this verse: "By pride comes only contention but with the well-advised is wisdom." Proverbs 13:10

Almighty God wants to Give you Victory!

God Almighty wants you to have victory over your pet sins and hang ups – not defeat! Don't you think it's time to repent and submit to His wisdom and His authority? Don't you realize that He knows better than you how you should be living your life? He created you for a purpose. He gave you your talents, abilities, and a unique blend of personality traits. Don't you think He knows best how to use those gifts to His glory and your eternal good? Isn't it time for you to take a hard look at the big picture? Won't you consider eternal values and consequences instead of your short-sighted pleasure and desires? Please consider these potent passages:

"Do not be deceived, God is not mocked; for whatever a man sows, that he will also reap. For he who sows to his flesh will of the flesh reap corruption, but he who sows to the Spirit will of the Spirit reap everlasting life." Galatians 6:7-8

"Beloved, I beg you as sojourners and pilgrims, abstain from fleshly lusts which war against the soul, having your conduct honorable among the Gentiles, that when they speak against you as evildoers, they may, by your good works which they observe, glorify God in the day of visitation." 1 Peter 2:11-12

"Likewise you younger people, submit yourselves to your elders. Yes, all of you be submissive to one another, and be clothed with humility, for 'God resists the proud, but gives grace to the humble.' Therefore humble yourselves under the mighty hand of God, that He may exalt you in due time, casting all your care upon Him, for He cares for you. Be sober, be vigilant; because your adversary the devil walks about like a roaring lion, seeking whom he may devour. Resist him, steadfast in the faith, knowing that the same sufferings are experienced by your brotherhood in the world." 1 Peter 5:5-9

"He who overcomes shall inherit all things, and I will be his God and he shall be My son. But the cowardly, unbelieving, abominable, murderers, sexually immoral, sorcerers, idolaters, and all liars shall have

their part in the lake which burns with fire and brimstone, which is the second death." Revelation 21:7-8

"You Shall Not Covet"

Has it ever occurred to you that the command of God, "You shall not covet," applies directly to the issues of cross-dressing and attempts to switch gender? Why? Because if you are dissatisfied with the gender God created you, then you end up coveting the type of body God did not give you.

Do you realize that coveting is idolatry? This is serious – very serious! *"Therefore put to death your members which are on the earth: fornication, uncleanness, passion, evil desire, and covetousness, which is idolatry."* Colossians 3:5. *"The wicked in his pride persecutes the poor;*

Let them be caught in the plots which they have devised. **For the wicked boasts of his heart's desire;** *he blesses the greedy and renounces the Lord."* Psalm 10:2-3. Coveting is desiring – longing for – something that belongs to someone else.

Griping – or Gratitude?

Do you realize that dissatisfaction with the sexuality God has given you is sinful discontent? If you are grumbling and complaining because you want to be a woman, but God made you a man, or that you want to be a man, yet God made you a woman, then you are guilty of ingratitude. This also is serious – very serious. God condemned the whole nation of Israel (with the only exceptions being Joshua and Caleb) to die in the wilderness because of their ingratitude, complaining, and lack of faith in Him. Paul, by inspiration, wrote: *"... because, although they knew God, they did not glorify Him as God, nor were thankful, but became futile in their thoughts, and their foolish hearts were darkened. ... Therefore God also gave them up to uncleanness, in the lusts of their hearts, to dishonor their bodies among themselves, who exchanged the truth of God for the lie, and worshiped and served the creature rather than the Creator, who is blessed forever. Amen.*" Romans 1:21, 24-25

Beware of the Father of Lies!

If you are struggling with the temptations I've described, be careful! Be on your guard! Satan is the father of lies. He is subtle and persistent. If you have been yielding to the temptations, you need to deeply and truly repent. If you choose instead to harden your heart and stiffen your neck in rebellion – beware!

The bottom line issue is sin. **Rebellion is like the sin of witchcraft! If you are not satisfied with the gender God gave you, you need to repent!** God tells you to "be content with such things as you have" – that includes body parts. Stop envying the members of the opposite sex and stop lusting after their body parts that you don't have because God didn't give them to you. Wake up and grow up! You can throw a tantrum and parade in the street spewing venom if you so choose – but it will not change the facts. *Recognize that confusion about your gender – whether you are male or female – is the ultimate confusion, and "God is NOT the author of confusion"!* 1 Corinthians 14:33

Who Is the Author of Confusion?

Who then is the author of confusion? Satan! **Who do you choose to follow – subtle Satan or conquering Christ? Christ is the conqueror of confusion.** Trust Him! Follow Him!

I'm thankful to be a man. That is who God created me to be. I don't wear earrings, frilly nightgowns, pink panties or a bra. By the way, Della is my wife and she does wear those things – for which I'm also thankful. There is enough confusion in the world without us adding to it. If what I've expressed makes me appear outdated – fine! I would much rather be outdated than rebellious. And if the fact that I don't want my tax dollars funding so-called "sex change surgeries" and I don't want some man who calls himself by a female name barging into a ladies' restroom, locker room or shower room shocking my wife, daughter, granddaughters or other flustered females makes me a bigot – so be it. Call me a bigot if you please. I can handle it. If you think I'm an outdated, uncouth, blunt bigot – that's okay. We still live in a country with the freedom of speech (in spite of those who want to steal it or squelch it). You can exercise your freedom of speech as I have mine. But please, please, while you are exercising your freedom of speech –speak to your Creator. **Ask Him, "Lord, what would You have me to do?" And please also read His Word – His wisdom. He will speak to you if you approach Him with an open heart. By His amazing grace He rescued me from my pit, and by His amazing grace He can rescue you from yours.**

Is Self-Identification Valid?

Often the excuse given by proponents of homosexual behavior - including cross-dressing and homosexual "marriage" – is self- identification. If a man feels more like a female than a male – does that make him a female? Should that give him the right and privilege to enter and use women's' restrooms and shower rooms? What makes you think he is not a male predator looking for his next victim while pretending to feel more like a female than a male? **Why are city municipalities bowing to such outrageous imbecility? Politically correct? NO! Politically, socially and morally insane!**

Also, if you get the impression that such cowardice on the part of government officials makes me angry – you are absolutely right! Sometimes anger toward evil, injustice, cowardice and outright moral stupidity is the most appropriate emotion for an individual who cares about truth, justice and righteousness. **Jesus got angry!** He drove out the wicked money changers from the temple. **The Word of God says, "Be angry – and sin not!"**

Anger in itself is not sin – but we must be careful how we handle it. I am expressing my anger in words and praying for positive change in society. I am not sending death threats or attacking anyone's person.

Why? *"For the weapons of our warfare are not carnal but mighty in God for pulling down strongholds, casting down arguments and every high thing that exalts itself against the knowledge of God, bringing every thought into captivity to the obedience of Christ,"* 2 Corinthians 10:4-5.

By the way, if a Caucasian man decides that he feels more like a black man, do you think our "politically correct" politicians will sign him up for affirmative action?

Also, the quote, "be content with such things as you have" is actually mentioned in the context of sexual purity versus impurity. Please notice for yourself. "Marriage is honorable among all, and the bed undefiled; but fornicators and adulterers God will judge. Let your conduct be without covetousness; *be content with such things as you have.* For He Himself has said, "I will never leave you nor forsake you." Hebrews 13:4-5.

Personal Convictions

I realize that part of what I am expressing is my own personal conviction and choice, which I do not bind on you as a doctrinal issue. I know of brothers in Christ who choose to wear long hair, earrings and tattoos, but are reaching souls for Christ. Some of them see their choice of style as a means of becoming "all things to all men that by all means I might win some". I praise God for their success in reaching souls for Christ, but still choose not to conform to the prevailing styles of our corrupt culture that complicates and confuses the distinctions between males and females. (By the way, tattoos were specifically mentioned and forbidden under the old covenant law, Leviticus 19:28, along with many other specific taboos under the law.) This is not an issue of law versus grace, but an issue of discernment and wisdom about how to relate to others in our corrupt culture, and how to wisely apply Biblical principles in our outreach. The flip side of conformity to culture in order to relate was also penned by Paul: *"I beseech you therefore, brethren, by the mercies of God, that you present your bodies a living sacrifice, holy, acceptable to God, which is your reasonable service.* **And do not be conformed to this world, but be transformed by the renewing of your mind,** *that you may prove what is that good and acceptable and perfect will of God."* Romans 12:1-2. The NLT of verse 2 reads: *"Don't copy the behavior and customs of this world, but let God transform you into a new person by changing the way you think. Then you will learn to know God's will for you, which is good and pleasing and perfect."*

I once asked a brother in Christ, "If you aren't trying to look like a woman, a pirate, or a rock singer, why wear an earring?" His reply was not too impressive, and I still believe it is a valid question. You have the right to wear long hair, earrings and pink panties if you want to, but if you choose to do so, I hope that you are a woman!

Who is Your Example?

A shining example of my major point is the Christian philosopher and evangelist, Ravi Zacharias, who speaks to multiplied thousands of college students each year on major campuses around the world. Ravi does not wear long hair, earrings, tattoos, or baggy pants to attempt to be relevant – yet there are overflowing crowds nearly every place he speaks. Why? He is a master communicator, who speaks truth in love and shows the relevance of the Word of God and the person of Jesus Christ to hurting hearts hungering for light, love, life, forgiveness, peace, truth, and joy. He dresses in a suit and does not conform to the world's wild styles, yet his message of the Master is winsome to multitudes. Let's go and do likewise!

I do also recognize the hard truth so candidly expressed by Chuck Swindoll: "God reserves the right to use people who disagree with me!" (Excerpted from "The Growth of an Expanding Mission," copyright © 1978 by Charles R. Swindoll, Inc. All rights reserved. Used by permission.) I do want to clarify that in sharing this quote from Chuck Swindoll I'm primarily referring to the disputable matters that Paul wrote about in Romans 14. These would be matters of opinion and conviction rather than matters of God's clear, distinct revelation of truth. However, it is also true that our creative Father even uses Satan and evil men to carry out His ultimate purposes - as He did at Calvary. Had they known and understood His plan they "would not have crucified the Lord of Glory." An ancient summary of Biblical convictions reads:

In essentials – unity

In opinions – liberty

In all things – charity

This is wise counsel – but often we still struggle with which things are essentials and which are opinions. That's when "in all things – charity" comes most into play.

Oh yes – I almost forgot to tell you that I **do** believe in gay marriage – if you look up the true meaning of the word "gay", before it became an intentionally warped word by those promoting the homosexual agenda. Now I prefer to call it merry marriage – one man and one woman committed to each other for life to love and serve God by loving and serving each other, their family, their church, their community, and their world. Am I still an outdated bigot?

"The greatest gift one generation can give to the next is a moral society." ~ Dietrich Bonhoeffer

"Gay Pride Parade"?

On Saturday, June 15, 2013, when I was walking, praying and distributing Christian literature along the Wilson Creek greenbelt trail near our home, a fellow believer asked me why I wasn't distributing the literature at the "Gay Pride Parade" over in Boise. The man told me that he is now divorced because his wife had rejected him to become a lesbian and that she was probably marching in that parade. Is that something to be proud of? What is it that she – and the other participants - are celebrating? He also told me about a Christian military man who was invited to speak briefly to a group of homosexuals as the representative of the "right wing" conservative Christians. He accepted their invitation. So what did he tell them? He said approximately the following: **"I'm not straight and you're not gay. We are all sinners in need of the grace of God!"** It's true! It cuts through the layers of lies, excuses, and blatant rebellion to get to the heart of the issue.

One of those deceptive lies that is perpetrated by so-called theologians who choose to practice homosexuality is that the sin of Sodom was the lack of compassion and hospitality to strangers. If you don't believe this is a blatant distortion of the Word of God, I challenge you to take a concordance and read every passage in Scripture about Sodom and sodomy. Here is one example: *"as Sodom and Gomorrah, and the cities around them in a similar manner to these, having given themselves over to sexual immorality and gone after strange flesh, are set forth as an example, suffering the vengeance of eternal fire."* Jude 7. In warning us about "ungodly men who turn the grace of God into licentiousness and deny the only Lord God and our Lord Jesus Christ", Jude further says, *"But these speak evil of whatever they do not know; and whatever they know naturally, like brute beasts, in these things they corrupt themselves. Woe to them! For they have gone in the way of Cain, have run greedily in the error of Balaam for profit, and perished in the rebellion of Korah."* Jude 10-11. What is the "way of Cain"? Cain was the one who could have sung, "I Did it My Way," when he offered to God a bloodless offering – the work of his own hands. When God confronted him with his wrongdoing and the sin lurking at his door, instead of conquering the temptation, Cain killed his brother. (Genesis 4:6-8). Beware of religious people who determine to do it their own way. Don't follow them because "I Did It My Way" could be the theme song of those on their way to hell. They may also decide to attack you if you dare to confront them. Confront them anyway. God did! Jesus did! The apostles did!

Later, on the radio, I heard a story about a "straight" Boy Scout leader who marched with the homosexuals in the Salt Lake City "Gay Pride Parade" in solidarity with their cause. **What a travesty! What**

a ludicrous distortion of truth and righteousness! Why does "a married man with children and a golden retriever" want solidarity with a parade of people who glory in their shame? Did the leaders of the homosexual agenda intentionally call people to demonstrate their rebellion against God? They oppose and mock God's standards by marching under the banner of attitudes and actions that God hates. See Genesis 19 (the story of Lot and the judgment of the cities of Sodom and Gomorrah).

1. The attitudes God hates are pride and rebellion, yet rebels who glory in their shame want to parade their pride.

2. The actions God hates are all forms of sexual immorality – that is, every form of sexual activity outside the marriage bond of one man with one woman. Adultery, fornication, bi-sexuality, homo-sexuality, pornography, bestiality, etc.

3. The other actions God hates are the practices of lying, twisting Scriptures, and distorting scientific research in vain attempts to justify polluted practices. The homosexual agenda is fueled and promoted by lies. Consider these pertinent passages of Scripture: *"These six things the Lord hates, Yes, seven are an **abomination** to Him: A proud look, A lying tongue, Hands that shed innocent blood, A heart that devises wicked plans, Feet that are swift in running to evil, A false witness who speaks lies, And one who sows discord among brethren."* Proverbs 6:16-19.

"Now the purpose of the commandment is love from a pure heart, from a good conscience, and from sincere faith, from which some, having strayed, have turned aside to idle talk, desiring to be teachers of the law, understanding neither what they say nor the things which they affirm. But we know that the law is good if one uses it lawfully, knowing this: that the law is not made for a righteous person, but for the lawless and insubordinate, for the ungodly and for sinners, for the unholy and pro-fane, for murderers of fathers and murderers of mothers, for manslayers, for fornicators, for sodomites, for kidnappers, for liars, for perjurers, and

if there is any other thing that is contrary to sound doctrine, according to the glorious gospel of the blessed God which was committed to my trust." 1Timothy 1:5-11.

Homosexual behavior is classified as an abomination in the Word of God. *"You shall not lie with a male as with a woman. It is an abomination."* Leviticus 18:22. As you may have noticed in the Proverbs 6 passage, **both a proud look and a lying tongue are also classified as "an abomination to Him,"** therefore God not only hates the attitude of pride that parades the shame of homosexual behavior, He hates practice of such degradation and the lies used to justify and promote it. **We are to have compassion on those trapped by any form of corruption or addiction, but how dare any Christian defy God by seeking to justify such ungodly practices?**

Proverbs 12:22 says, "Lying lips are an abomination to the Lord, but those who deal truthfully are His delight."

Is Homosexual Sin a Civil Right?

"They're equating their sin with my skin." (Dwight McKissic of Arlington, Texas, who is black, on efforts to compare same-sex marriage to the civil-rights movement. The Blaze, June 21, 2012)

Born that Way?

Please do not hit me with the old worn-out lie that homosexuals are "born that way and it is impossible to change their orientation". The fact is that every last one of us is born with a corrupted sinful nature which is attracted to sin like iron to a magnet. We are all by nature "children of wrath" – "without God and without hope in this world" because we are all children of our original parents, Adam and Eve. We live on a cursed earth because of their rebellion – their sin – in violating God's one restriction on their freedom. Eve chose to believe Satan's lie over God's truth, and Adam chose to sin with Eve, rather than to stand alone with God for truth and righteousness. Now, rather than wasting your time blaming them for your condition, it will be far better and more profitable to believe the Word of God that you are yourself a sinful rebel. *"For there is no difference, for all have sinned and come short of the glory of God."* Romans 6:22-23. "There is none righteous, no not one". In fact, the prophet Jeremiah by inspiration wrote, *"The heart is deceitful above all things, and desperately wicked. Who can know it? I, the Lord, search the heart, I test the mind, even to give every man according to His ways, and according to the fruit of his doings."* Jeremiah 17:9-10. What are you going to say when you stand before the judgment bar of Almighty God and see every thought, motive and action of your entire life? *"For the word of God is living and powerful, and sharper than any two-edged sword, piercing even to the division of soul and spirit, and of joints and marrow, and is a discerner of the thoughts and intents of the heart. And there is no creature hidden from His sight, but all things are naked and open to the eyes of Him to whom we must give account."* Hebrews 4:12-13. I don't want justice – I want grace! What about you? I have accepted the grace of God – for my penalty was paid for by the blood of my Lord Jesus Christ. What about you?

How do You Handle Criticism?
(Humbly Listening or Proudly Rejecting?)

Friend, how do you handle criticism – by humbly listening or proudly rejecting? Will you be wise enough to honestly, humbly consider these passages from God's wisdom literature?

"He who corrects a scoffer gets shame for himself, and he who rebukes a wicked man only harms himself. Do not correct a scoffer, lest he hate you; rebuke a wise man, and he will love you. Give instruction to a wise man, and he will be still wiser; teach a just man, and he will increase in learning. 'The fear of the Lord is the beginning of wisdom, and the knowledge of the Holy One is understanding'. . . Open rebuke is better than love carefully concealed. Faithful are the wounds of a friend, but the kisses of an enemy are deceitful." Proverbs 9:7-10, 27:5-6

"It is better to hear the rebuke of the wise than for a man to hear the song of fools." Ecclesiastes 7:5

Good by Nature?

Just think about it! Do you really believe that we human beings are born good by nature? If so, why do parents have to diligently teach their children to share instead of being selfish; to tell the truth rather than telling lies to protect self? Indeed, "They go forth from the womb speaking lies." Psalm 58:3. The fact is that we are all by nature stubborn, selfish, sinful rebels. That's why we need to be born anew from above – to receive a new nature given to us by our gracious God, Who then uses our experiences to mold us into the image of His Son, our Lord Jesus Christ.

It is true that God created human beings good by nature – but they did not stay that way. On the sixth day, after He had created human beings "male and female", He declared his creation "very good." This is proof positive that sex and sexuality are not inherently evil. Sexuality is by God's creation a beautiful gift from our Creator to be handled with care and celebrated in marriage and family.

The reason human beings are no longer good by nature is that rebellion against God by our original parents changed everything, and brought a curse on earth. Their nature was corrupted by sin, and that corrupted nature has been the inheritance of every human being. Sin has consequences – terrible consequences that affect other people. It was true for Adam and Eve – it is true for us!

"Those Christians Are Always Putting People Down!"

How should we who are dedicated Christians reply to the above accusation? I don't know about you, but I will ask the one making this assertion, "My friend, aren't you a bit confused? In fact – aren't you very confused? Wouldn't you agree that someone who doesn't know up from down is confused – very confused? We don't need to put people down – they are already down. All human beings struggle with our selfish, depraved nature. If you will read the New Testament with an open, inquiring mind you will find that Jesus was consistently lifting up those who were down – except for the hypocrites who were putting others down and exalting themselves. By the way, I have three more questions for you:

1. Isn't your statement, 'Those Christians are always putting people down,' self-defeating? If you don't like someone who is putting other people down, what about you? Aren't you putting down Christians (at least your caricature of Christians)?

2. Do you actually believe in your heart of hearts that naming sin as sinful is the same as putting people down? Do you not love your own children while telling them that lying, cheating and stealing are wrong while lifting them up from these sins and forgiving them for their failures?

3. What are you doing with your own guilt? The arms of Jesus are open to you if you come to Him in genuine repentance. Also, true Christians will receive you, forgive you, and lift you up when you honestly admit your own guilt and depravity."

Now I want to share with you a portion of Ravi Zacharias' comments following the terrorist attacks in Paris, France on Friday, November 13, 2015. His column was titled, "Is Paris Burning?"

"It would be easy to lose heart and become cynical. But No! There is One who sees all things, knows all things, and will ultimately triumph over all things. There is only one message that addresses the truth as the truth. The Lord of glory, Jesus Christ, came to this earth and was also the victim of hate. Lies sent him to the cross. Power overruled reality, as politics and religious demagogues once again made the lie seem noble. But the Lord who sees the beginning from the end amazingly conquered not in spite of the dark mystery of evil, rather, He conquered through it. James Stewart of Scotland, pointing to the cross, said it in the most powerful terms I have read. Commenting on the verse from Psalm 68:18, 'He led captivity captive,' he said,

It is a glorious phrase—'He led captivity captive.' The very triumphs of his foes, it means, he used for their defeat. He compelled their dark achievements to subserve his ends not theirs. They nailed Him to a tree, not knowing that by that very act they were bringing the world to His feet. They gave Him a cross, not guessing that He would make it a throne. They flung Him outside the city gates to die, not knowing that in that very moment they were lifting up the gates of the universe, to let the King come in. They thought to root out His doctrines, not understanding that they were implanting imperishably in the hearts of men the very name they intended to destroy. They thought they had God with His back to the wall, pinned helpless and defeated: they did not know that it was God himself who had tracked them down. He did not conquer in spite of the dark mystery of evil. He conquered *through* it.' (James Stewart quote is in public domain.)

The lie has a shelf life. The truth abides forever. God can even conquer through our perversion.

One more thing. I would be remiss if I left the guilt and darkness out there. That is the seduction of a fake righteousness. We all have to look at our own hearts and see the evil that is within each one of us. Only then can we find the answer from which all other answers flow. Some time ago, I was in Romania. A sculptor had some of his works on display. One was a horrific, fierce-looking, long nail. When you picked it up, as rusty and jagged as the nail was, the head was polished and shiny. And when you looked at that polished head, you saw a reflection of yourself. It is sobering. Very sobering.

You see, the nails that cause hurt and pain and death ultimately point to our own hearts. Only when we as individuals see the evil that is within will we find an answer for the evil that is around us. Maybe, just maybe, someday a carnage will take place that might cause everyone in power to see their own hearts as God sees them and tell us the truth of what these killings are all about. Only then will truth triumph and we find real answers. Until then, the flames will gain ground and not just Paris will burn, but the next story of scorched lives in another city will make us forget this one… or possibly, awaken us to the cost of a lie. More than ever we need the Savior. Lord have mercy!"

~ Ravi Zacharias (© 2011 Ravi Zacharias International Ministries and/or its suppliers. All rights reserved. Used by permission.)

Warning!

There is a Baptist preacher who travels to homosexual events with a few followers in order to shout denunciations and carry signs like, "God Hates Fags". This man is a renegade and a false teacher. He does not "speak the truth in love" as the Word of God teaches (commands), so he is not a representative of Biblical Christianity and does not represent Baptists. He and his followers are a shame and reproach to the cause of Christ – as are any others who choose to use his tactics. We are to "expose the unfruitful works of darkness" – but not with the hateful, ungodly tactics he uses. Likewise, those who claim to be pro-life, yet take the law into their own hands by killing abortion doctors (or attempting to do so) are not representing Biblical Christianity. They also are distorting truth and righteousness. What if the early Christians had murdered Saul of Tarsus in retaliation for his ungodly persecution? They would have killed the man God planned to transform into the apostle Paul!

Is it Possible to Change?

Is it possible for human beings to change - to deny self and sinful temptations instead of soaking in sinful self-indulgence (whether lust, greed, envy or perverted attractions toward homosexuality, bestiality, child pornography, etc.)? Yes! Definitely! *"For the grace of God that brings salvation has appeared to all men, teaching us that, denying ungodliness and worldly lusts, we should live soberly, righteously, and godly in the present age, looking for the blessed hope and glorious appearing of our great God and Savior Jesus Christ."* Titus 2:11-13. I am personally a converted liar, luster and lover of pleasure rather than a lover of God. I personally know many converted addicts – who were hooked on drugs, alcohol, and pornography – **but now love God more than their sinful inclinations.** I know personally two converted homosexuals – and have heard testimonies of many others who no longer yield to their sinful inclinations. One of them lives here locally and is married with a family. Don't try to convince me that homosexuality is a genetic condition – like skin color – that cannot be changed. I have also personally heard black people who repudiate and despise the agenda of homosexuals who claim their "civil rights" on the basis of the civil rights of black people. I know ex-homosexuals, but I don't know any ex-black people! Do you? Be honest! Admit that the claim that homosexuals "were born that way and cannot change" is planned propaganda. Thank you!

I know of a church in Colorado that cares enough for confused people to train them how to act properly. There was a man in their congregation who was **not** a homosexual, but who gave the impression of such because many of his actions and mannerisms reflected feminine traits. Why? He lacked masculine mentors in his family, so from a small child he had learned to mimic the mannerisms of his mother and sisters. That is probably a major factor with many boys growing up in single mother families where they do not have a father image to be a model for them of how to act like a man. The men in the congregation cared enough for this man to speak the truth in love to him about his feminine looking mannerisms and mentored him in how to think, walk, talk and act like a man. Friends – this is love in action! They did not mock him. They did not whisper about him or gossip about him. They mentored him. Let's go and do likewise!

Friends, God loves you just as you are – but He loves you too much to allow you to stay that way. That is how Christians are to love one another. It is also how we are to love our opponents – our enemies who hate who we are and what we stand for. Please consider, *"For God so loved the world that He gave His only begotten Son, that whoever believes in Him should not perish but have everlasting life."* John 3:16 – then, *"By this we know love, because He laid down His life for us. And we also ought to lay down our lives for the brethren."* 1 John 3:16.

Now look at something else John wrote in his epistle of love in action – *"Now by this we know that we know Him, if we keep His commandments. He who says, 'I know Him,' and does not keep His commandments, is a liar, and the truth is not in him. But whoever keeps His word, truly the love of God is perfected in him. By this we know that we are in Him. He who says he abides in Him ought himself also to walk just as He walked. Brethren, I write no new commandment to you, but an old commandment which you have had from the beginning. The old commandment is the word which you heard from the beginning. Again, a new commandment I write to you, which thing is true in Him and in you, because the darkness is passing away, and the true light is already shining. He who says he is in the light, and hates his brother, is in darkness until now. He who loves his brother abides in the light, and there is no cause for stumbling in him. But he who hates his brother is in darkness and walks in darkness, and does not know where he is going, because the darkness has blinded his eyes. . . Do not love the world or the things in the world. If anyone loves the world, the love of the Father is not in him. For all that is in the world—the lust of the flesh, the lust of the eyes, and the pride of life—is not of the Father but is of the world. And the world is passing away, and the lust of it; but he who does the will of God abides forever."* 1 John 2:3-11, 15-17. Friends, as another brother put it succinctly, **"I'm not who I want to be, and I'm not who I'm going to be, but thank God I'm not who I used to be!" Can you also say that?**

Why Do Christians Strongly Reject Racial Discrimination

Yet Discriminate Against Those With Different Sexual Orientations?

A female journalist came to see and hear Ravi Zacharias at one of his speaking appointments. She had intended to only stay for ten minutes, but became enthralled with his presentation and stayed for the entire lecture, plus question and answer time - over two hours. Later she spoke with him personally and requested permission to ask more questions. As they were leaving the site, she walked beside him and asked the question in the heading above. His answer was both concise and brilliant. He told her that the answer is consistent with Biblical convictions. It is both simple and clear. Almighty God created human beings in His own image, and He created them male and female.

Within the DNA and genetics of human beings (and many of God's other creatures) is a vast propensity for variety. Now, after thousands of years to "be fruitful and multiply" as God commanded Adam and Eve, human beings exist in many ethnic varieties - but all human beings were created in the image of God and bear the image of their Maker. Human life is sacred because all human beings bear that image. For some human beings to mock or mistreat other human beings because they outwardly have a few different design features is to mock and mistreat what God has made sacred. Sexuality is also sacred. The Heavenly Father Himself created them male and female and created one woman for one man for life. (He did allow for divorce under very restricted conditions. God Himself gave His unfaithful wife, Israel, a bill of divorce. Jeremiah 3:6-8)

He is the author of marriage and family. No court, no culture, no conference of rebellious human beings has the right to mock, mistreat, misuse or attempt to redefine marriage. Sexuality is God's creation and is sacred. The seventh of God's Ten Commandments is: "You shall not commit adultery." (Exodus 10:14). Any and all sexual practices outside of God's design for sexual love between a husband and his wife are wrong, because they violate the sacredness of sexuality as ordained by Almighty God. Homosexuality is specifically named and identified by God as an abomination. (Leviticus 18:22; Romans 1:22-32; 1 Corinthians 6:9-11).

Is Discrimination Always Wrong?

The word "discriminate" means to make a distinction between one thing and another; to make a judgment, to distinguish. Everyone discriminates. It is impossible to live without making any judgments. Why? Because some things are good and some evil; some are wise and some are foolish; some are true and some are false. Ironically, often those who rail against Christians for discrimination do so while calling them bigots, intolerant, hateful or much worse! Isn't that something like spitting against the wind?

To discriminate in one sense of its meaning is to discern. It is not wrong to discriminate against an idea, doctrine, or practice that is wrong or hurtful to ourselves or others. In fact, to practice wisdom we must be discerning – that is – to discriminate against ideas or practices that are evil, especially those that are specifically named as evil in the Word of God. (There are some things that are evil which we must discern as such by applying Biblical principles.)

On the other hand, if we use the word discriminate to mean mocking or mistreating other human beings, it is wrong. The Word of God says: "Let **no corrupt word** proceed out of your mouth, but **what is good for necessary edification, that it may impart grace to the hearers. And do not grieve the Holy Spirit** of God, by whom you were sealed for the day of redemption. **Let all bitterness, wrath, anger, clamor, and evil speaking be put away from you, with all malice.**" Ephesians 4:29-31. If we, who profess to be representing our Lord Jesus Christ, are jeering at other human beings and calling them derogatory names for their ungodly practices, then we are guilty of violating the above commands and woefully misrepresenting Jesus, Who was known as the Friend of sinners. We need to remember the pit from which we were dug and repent. Paul instructed Timothy, **"Flee also youthful lusts; but pursue righteousness, faith, love, peace with those who call on the Lord out of a pure heart.** But avoid foolish and ignorant disputes, knowing that they generate strife. **And a servant of the Lord must not quarrel but be gentle to all, able to teach, patient, in humility correcting those who are in opposition, if God perhaps will grant them repentance, so that they may know the truth, and** *that* **they may come to their senses** *and escape* **the snare of the devil,** having been taken captive by him to do his will." 2 Timothy 2:22-26.

Clarification and Conclusion

It is wrong to discriminate against any person for his ethnicity because his ethnicity is sacred. Why sacred? Because every human being is created in the image of God – and ethnicity is an integral part of being human.

It is wrong to discriminate against Christians for standing strong for Biblical truth about sexuality. Why? Because sexuality is sacred. Why sacred? Because God Himself created sexuality when He created human beings as male and female. Marriage between a man and woman is sacred. Why? Because Almighty God, the inventor of sex and sexuality, ordained marriage to be between one man and one woman with the primary purpose being to "be fruitful and multiply" – and more specifically to produce "godly offspring." (Malachi 2:15). Misusing sex for purposes other than what is ordained and specified by the Inventor of human beings and human sexuality is wrong, rebellious and sinful. (Note: The Song of Solomon plus other portions of Scripture also clarify that sexual pleasure inside the covenant of marriage and companionship are also among God's purposes for marriage.)

Thankfully I can report that the female journalist listened carefully to Ravi's answer to her probing question and then said softly, "I never thought of it that way before!" I thank God that she not only posed a "hard question" to Ravi, but that she actually listened to and thought about his logical answer. Are you open and willing to do the same?

The Bottom-Line Problem

In reality, the question the journalist asked shows a serious lack of discernment. Why? Because she failed to discern the obvious difference between ethnicity and rebellion. Ethnicity is an integral, unchangeable trait of every human being. Rebellion against God's pattern for sexuality produces sexual practices that violate God's pattern. Those practices are the result of bad choices and are not an integral part of who I am or who you are, contrary to the mantra of the homosexual activists. We can repent. We can change – and multiplied thousands of Christians can testify to the fact of transformed lives.

The Solution

The solution is to recognize and believe that Jesus did not come to earth to wage war against men – but against sin. Will you choose to accept Him, His forgiveness and His solution, and love Him more than you love sin?

Struggles and Temptations

Every human being struggles with temptations. In fact, the struggle increases after committing to follow Christ for two reasons:

1. Before surrendering your life to Jesus, you were more inclined to surrender to temptation than to resist it.

2. There is an enemy to our souls – Satan – and spiritual warfare is real – often intense. He wants to recapture you.

However, not only is there hope – there is certain victory in Christ. **"In Christ" is the key factor.** Abide in Christ! Focus on Christ! Walk with Christ. "For whatever is born of God overcomes the world. And this is the victory that has overcome the world—our faith." 1 John 5:4

It is a good idea to saturate your mind with the powerful truths in Romans chapter 6, 7 and 8.

Chapter 6. My old man of sin died with Christ, was buried in baptism, and I am now a new man raised with Christ.

Chapter 7. My new man of righteousness in Christ is haunted by the old man of sin who seems to have more lives than a cat. Scat cat! Go back to the grave where you belong!

Chapter 8. I am a new man in Christ! I am inhabited, possessed, and empowered by His Holy Spirit. I have nothing to fear – not even fear itself. Why not? **Because in Christ I am more than a conqueror!** That is my identity.

Some recovery programs have the participants stand up in front each session and make a false confession – at least for those in Christ. Each one is to say, "I am an alcoholic" or "I am a sex addict", etc. NO! If you are **in Christ** that is **NOT** who you are! **Don't dwell on who you were – focus on who you are.** Isn't it much better to say, "Satan is after me"? He is persistent with temptations – but we buried my old man. **I am a new man in Christ! I am more than a conqueror!"**

I have trusted Christ for forgiveness and salvation – I can trust Him for victory over my addictions, my hang-ups and my pet sins, as well as my irritations, aggravations and frustrations. I don't need to lose my cool! I don't need to blow my stack! I don't need to try to drown my sorrows in alcohol! In my core being, my spirit, I am a child of the King. His Spirit lives inside my spirit. I AM MORE THAN A CONQUEROR!

What will it look like in your life if you truly believe that you are MORE THAN A CONQUEROR? Who can thwart you? What can stop you when you are MORE THAN A CONQUEROR?!

If you are struggling with homosexual temptations or tendencies, I highly recommend that you consider reading these articles:

1. "Sodom more than a gay issue...", by Ed Vitagliano (*AFA Journal,* June 2013, pgs. 16-17, www.afajournal. org)

2. "Journey of Grace: From lesbianism to the parking lot of church. An interview with author Rosaria Butterfield", from *World Magazine*, by Marvin Olasky (Samaritan Ministries, May 2013, *Christian Health Care Newsletter*)

3. "No Truth Without Love – No Love Without Truth", by Dr. Albert Mohler (*Eternal Perspectives*, Summer Issue 2013)

Know When to Fight and When to Flee!

Being more than a conqueror in spiritual warfare involves the wisdom of knowing when to fight and when to flee. We are to confront evil and fight the good fight by exposing the works of darkness with the light.

However, when Satan's strategy involves sexual temptations, the wisdom of God mandates flight instead of fight! "*Flee sexual immorality. Every sin that a man does is outside the body, but he who commits sexual immorality sins against his own body*" 1 Corinthians 6:18. "*Flee also youthful lusts; but pursue righteousness, faith, love, peace with those who call on the Lord out of a pure heart.*" 2 Timothy 2:22

"*...I want you to be wise in what is good, and simple concerning evil. And the God of peace will crush Satan under your feet shortly. The grace of our Lord Jesus Christ be with you. Amen.*" Romans 16:19b-20. To bring balance to these exhortations (commands) to flee from sexual temptation and to be wise in waiting for Him to crush Satan under our feet, let us also never forget these powerful commands from God's inspired Word: " *Watch, stand fast in the faith, be brave, be strong. Let all that you do be done with love.*" 1 Corinthians 16:13-14

God's Intelligent Design for Marriage

I.   Unity in Diversity = Male plus Female

II. Recreation plus Procreation = Fun and Family

III. Transformation though Conflict Resolution = Character Development

God's Intelligent Design for Child Training

I.   Father and Mother – To Demonstrate and Train Children Godly Masculinity and Femininity

II. Tough and Tender Love

III. Discipleship through praise, encouragement and reward for good behavior and loving correction and punishment for bad behavior.

Appropriate Corrections, Encouragements, Rewards and Punishments.

Carefully study the Book of Proverbs for wisdom and balance in these important matters.

Homophobia

Homophobia is a made-up word that homosexual activists use to intimidate those who disagree with their agenda. Do I fear being accused of being homophobic? No! Absolutely not! Why not? First of all, I don't care what homosexual activists and their "liberal" colleagues choose to call me. Second, I freely admit that I do fear the unbridled corruption that homosexual activists are pushing off on our culture. Do you realize that historically there has never been a culture (society) that has continued to survive after labeling homosexual behavior as normal? So yes, I do fear for what is happening to our country – and especially to our youth. They are constantly being brainwashed through the public schools and the media with the propaganda that homosexuality is normal, acceptable, and to be celebrated. (Never mind the disease and death it is inflicting on millions worldwide!)

Some of the recent laws promoting their propaganda deserve the label of asinine. For example, consider this item from the June 9, 2013 issue of *The Times and the Scriptures:*

"State ordering girls' locker rooms open to boys"
(FROM ZIONICA, 5-14-13)

The California State Assembly passed a bill [last month] mandating that schools permit boys to play on girls' athletic teams and utilize the ladies' locker room if they "gender identify" as girls – or vice-versa for girls identifying as boys.

Read more: http://zionica.com/2013/05/14/state-ordering- girls-locker-rooms-open-to-boys/#ixzz2U4WroB6T

For discussion: Are the "shame" of Isa. 47:1-3 and the "modestly and discreetly" of 1 Tim. 2:9 too outdated to apply to 21st century co-ed showers? Or are we really supposed to accept this new "transgender" category as legitimate and worthy of special rights?" ("The Times and the Scriptures," Summer Supplement for June 9, 2013. Used by permission.)

Is it possible for legislators to pass a more outrageous law? My wife, Della, doesn't like for me to use the term asinine, but sometimes it is the most valid description of the insanity gripping our nation – and our world. (Asinine literally means stupid, silly, or unintelligent – but it carries a stronger punch than any of those terms.) So if you like the law passed by the legislators in California, and want to call me "homophobic" – go ahead. I might choose to wear it as a badge of honor.

By the way, are we so naïve that we don't believe that curious teen boys will now pretend to become transgender to gain access to girls' locker rooms? Do you trust those declared homosexuals who are already cross-dressers to be in the locker rooms with your daughters and granddaughters (or girls going into boys' locker rooms pretending to be gender-identity boys)?

There is a third reason why I don't fear being accused of being homophobic. It is because TRUTH WALKS UNAFRAID. What I'm sharing is the truth of God both from His infallible Word and from scientific research about the dangers of homosexuality. I do not fear cross examination.

Truth invites investigation!
Truth welcomes examination!
Truth rejects contamination!
TRUTH WALKS UNAFRAID!

Recently I saw a sticker that says, "Trust Your Heart." This expresses the warped wisdom of the world. God in His wisdom tells us, "GUARD YOUR HEART!" Why do I need to guard my heart? Here are three portions of the Word of God that clearly tell me why:

1. *"Keep your heart with all diligence, for out of it spring the issues of life."* Proverbs 4:23.

2. *"O Lord, I know the way of man is not in himself; It is not in man who walks to direct his own steps."* Jeremiah 10:23.

3. *"The heart is deceitful above all things, and desperately wicked; Who can know it?"* Jeremiah 17:9.

My friend, if you are feeling the temptation to submit to the powerful pressure of the homosexual propaganda and intimidation steamroller – GUARD YOUR HEART! Remember: *"No temptation has overtaken you except such as is common to man; but God is faithful, who will not allow you to be tempted beyond what you are able, but with the temptation will also make the way of escape, that you may be able to bear it. . ... Therefore, whether you eat or drink, or whatever you do, do all to the glory of God."* 1 Corinthians 10:13, 31

The Proper Role of Family, Church, and State

Almighty God is the Creator and Master of family, church, and state. He designed each of these institutions carefully with a different role to play in an orderly society. Each is a minister (servant) for the Master – and answerable to Him.

The Bottom Line

"Yet in all these things we are more than conquerors through Him

who loved us. For I am persuaded that neither death nor life, nor angels nor principalities nor powers, nor things present nor things to come, nor height nor depth, nor any other created thing, shall be able to separate us from the love of God which is in Christ Jesus our Lord." Romans 8:37-39

"For God has not given us a spirit of fear, but of power and of love and of a sound mind." 2 Timothy 1:7. Courage is not the absence of fear – it is the conquering of fear! You will not be inhibited by fear if you are inhabited by the Holy Spirit. **We are more than conquerors through Him who loved us.**

WE MUST BE COURTEOUS – BUT WE WILL NOT BE QUIET!

Potent Prayer

Lord, please fill me with Your Spirit and put me in the right place at the right time with the right words to honor You. Please give me the courage to confront and the grace to be courteous in the midst of our corrupted culture.

As you pray, remember that there are basically three kinds of people:

1. Those who are afraid.

2. Those who don't know enough to be afraid (the naïve).

3. Those who choose to trust God and believe His promises.

Supplement 1 – Highly Recommended Items

I highly recommend that you read these articles:

"Blurring the Lines": From haute couture to elementary schools, activists aren't just trying to 'push the envelope' when it comes to gender distinction – they're trying to erase the line, by Jeff Johnston. Visit CitizenLink.com: http://bit.ly/zafcj6 (Citizen Magazine, April 2012)

"No Truth Without Love – No Love Without Truth", by Dr. Albert Mohler. Dr. R. Albert Mohler Jr. (www.albertmohler.com) serves as president of The Southern Baptist Theological Seminary. Widely sought as a columnist and commentator, Dr. Mohler has been quoted in the nation's leading newspapers. (Eternal Perspectives, Summer 2013)

"Piercing the Gay Paradigm", by Ed Vitagliano (afaJournal, September 2013) www.afajournal.org

"Sodom", by Ed Vitaliano (afaJournal, June 2013) www.afajournal.org

ATTENTION!

The primary reason for the conflict over homosexuality among those who claim to be Christians is that those pushing perversion have forsaken the infallible Word of God as their standard. They are putting their faith in their feelings, rather than in the Truth of what God says. Unbelief is not weakness - it is wickedness!

Supplement 2

"It's gotten so bad we have to (try to) pass a law that says this?"
Reprinted from Breaking Christian news, 9-25-13

"A bill sponsored in the U.S. House of Representatives strives to guarantee that tax exempt status would not be threatened by beliefs contrary to the recently mandated redefinition of marriage.

Noting the reasons for the Marriage and Religious bill, Rep. Raul Labrador (R-ID) said: 'Regardless of your ideology, we can all agree about the importance of religious liberty. Our bill will protect freedom of conscience for those who believe marriage is the union of one man and one woman...'

Rep. Steve Scalise (R-LA) said, 'Recent legal challenges to Christians who refuse to provide services for homosexual weddings have caused alarm around the country. Furthermore, the Supreme Court's ruling on marriage may embolden those in government who want to impose their views of marriage on faith-based organizations. We need this legislation to protect freedom of conscience for those who believe marriage is the union of one man and one woman."' By Napp Nazworth, the Christian Post Reporter, summarized by Teresa Neumann.

"First annual 'Ex-Gay Awareness Month' awards are announced"
Reprinted from Family Research Council 10-2-13
(www.frc.org, 1-800-225-4008, 801 G Street,
NW, Washington, D.C. 20001)

"Monday night, the Washington, D.C. area was the site of the First Annual Ex-Gay Awareness Month Dinner and Reception. Threats to the civil rights of those who have abandoned a 'gay' identity and left the homosexual lifestyle, as well as those who have unwanted same-sex attractions and seek help to overcome them, have never been greater than they are now. Two states, California and New Jersey, have passed laws unprecedented in the history of psychology, to actually outlaw sexual orientation therapy with minors by licensed counselors.

Mat Staver of Liberty Counsel received the 'Ex-Gay Freedom Award' for his lawsuits challenging both statutes -- in fact, he left directly from the dinner for Trenton, New Jersey, to argue the case against the New Jersey law in federal district court yesterday morning. A pincer movement is underway in New Jersey – in addition to the new law restricting therapy with minors, a lawsuit by the Southern Poverty Law Center (SPLC) has charged both licensed and unlicensed counselors with 'consumer fraud.' Jews Offering New Alternatives for Healing (JONAH) is being defended by the Freedom of Conscience Defense Fund (FCDF), but the pro-homosexual activists are pursuing legal tactics that could bankrupt both organizations.

Dennis Jernigan, an ex-gay who is a renowned Christian musician (he wrote 'You Are My All in All' and other popular praise songs), provided music, while Trace McNutt, a former satanic drag queen, was winner of the 'Courage Award' for former homosexuals. The event was inspiring evidence that for homosexuals, change is possible – a message they have a right to hear.

To help these courageous allies, go to Jonahweb.org for JONAH and ActRight.com for FCDF. (Copyright 2013, *The Times and the Scriptures*, 948 Darlene Ave, Springfield, OR 97477, www.timesandscriptures.org. Weekly Bulletin for October 6, 2013. Used by permission.)

Supplement 3

Letter to a Boise State University Student

Dear Friend,

Does the fact that Tom Cruise is handsome and he has a gift of acting make him a scholar or authority about faith, truth, and what is good and evil?

Almighty God inspired Isaiah to write: ***"Woe to those who call evil good and good evil; who put darkness for light and light for darkness; who put bitter for sweet and sweet for bitter! Woe to those who are wise in their own eyes, and prudent in their own sight."*** Isaiah 5:20-21. Please carefully think and pray about what Ron Hubbard (founder of Scientology) said and wrote in contrast to God's Word.

Also, think and pray about what our corrupt culture says about homosexuality (which they choose to call "gay"), then read and pray about what God inspired in Romans 1:16-32 and 1 Corinthians 6:9-11 It was God Almighty Himself who designed and created Adam and Eve as male and female. God is the inventor of sexuality – and He designed it to be sacred, sanctified sexuality – as the foundation of marriage and family. Family is His design – and every child needs and desires to have both a Mommy and a Daddy. Marriage is the sacred union of one man with one woman in a sanctified covenant before God with one primary purpose being to produce godly offspring. Satan, the enemy of God and of our souls, seeks to steal, kill, and destroy the beauty of sacred, sanctified sexuality by perverting it into selfish, sordid sexuality. Whenever we yield to his temptation to indulge our minds or bodies in his cheap substitutes – remember "your sin will find you out." Satan wins and we lose our joy and destroy the beauty of

God's design. Praise God that He forgives, heals and restores!

"Yet you say, 'For what reason?' Because the LORD has been witness between you and the wife of your youth, with whom you have dealt treacherously; yet she is your companion and your wife by covenant. But did He not make them one, having a remnant of the Spirit? And why one? He seeks godly offspring. Therefore take heed to your spirit, and let none deal treacherously with the wife of his youth. 'For the LORD God of Israel says that He hates divorce, for it covers one's garment with violence,' says the LORD of hosts. 'Therefore take heed to your spirit, that you do not deal treacherously.' You have wearied the LORD with your words; yet you say, 'In what way have we wearied Him?' In that you say, 'Everyone who does evil is good in the sight of the LORD, and He delights in them,' Or, 'Where is the God of justice?'" Malachi 2:14-17

Homosexuality is a perversion of God's design for sacred, sanctified sexuality, but it is not the only perversion. Fornication, adultery, pedophilia, and bestiality are other forms of perversion that come under the condemnation rather than the blessing of Almighty God. Consider these passages:

"Do you not know that the unrighteous will not inherit the kingdom of God? Do not be deceived. Neither fornicators, nor idolaters, nor adulterers, nor homosexuals, nor sodomites, nor thieves, nor covetous, nor drunkards, nor revilers, nor extortioners will inherit the kingdom of God. And such were some of you. But you were washed, but you were sanctified, but you were justified in the name of the Lord Jesus and by the Spirit of our God." 1 Corinthians 6:9-11

"Marriage is honorable among all, and the bed undefiled; but fornicators and adulterers God will judge." Hebrews 13:4

"For the word of God is living and powerful, and sharper than any two-edged sword, piercing even to the division of soul and spirit, and of joints and marrow, and is a discerner of the thoughts and intents of the heart. And there is no creature hidden from His sight, but all things are naked and open to the eyes of Him to whom we must give account." Hebrews 4:12-13

"And He said to me, 'It is done! I am the Alpha and the Omega, the Beginning and the End. I will give of the fountain of the water of life freely to him who thirsts. He who overcomes shall inherit all things, and I will be his God and he shall be My son. But the cowardly, unbelieving, abominable, murderers, sexually immoral, sorcerers, idolaters, and all liars shall have their part in the lake which burns with fire and brimstone, which is the second death.'" Revelation 21:6-8.

God has created us in His own image and has given us with His sacred image the power and privilege of choice. You can choose to receive Jesus' payment for your sin by His sacrifice on the cross, be forgiven and drink of the fountain of the water of life – or you can reject His grace and have your part in the lake which burns with fire and brimstone. **His arms are open to you and He has already paid your penalty – do you choose to receive Him, or do you choose to receive the consequences of your sin – hell? It's your move!**

Yours & His,
Rick

P.S. I realize that those promoting the homosexual agenda (that is so powerfully influencing our corrupted culture) strongly rely on the intimidation tactics of name calling toward those of us who stand for the Biblical truth about marriage and homosexuality. They insist on using the terminology such as "homophobe"! "Bigot!" "Hateful!" I don't hate homosexuals, but I do hate what God hates – sin. I don't hate liars, but I hate to be lied to or lied about – don't you? All of us are guilty of lying (as well as most other sins), but Jesus loved us enough to die for us. Does that touch your heart? Your soul?

So if you choose Jesus, you may also be called those derogatory names. So what? Jesus said, "If they hated Me, they will hate you." You have to choose who you want to please – our corrupt culture or God our Loving Father.

By the way, there are some Christians (or professed Christians) led by a renegade Baptist pastor who travel around the country spewing out their hatred for homosexuals at "gay pride" parades and even funerals. They have degenerated to the level of the enemy of our souls by adopting the same tactic of name calling and severe denunciation that the homosexual activists use. Of course many "liberal" media outlets focus on the small band of renegades to give the impression that many or most Christians are like that. The Word of God does teach us to hate the sin yet love the sinner. Most of the Christians I know do practice this – or pray to be able to do so by His power. Jesus taught us: *"Blessed are the peacemakers, For they shall be called sons of God. Blessed are those who are persecuted for righteousness' sake, For theirs is the kingdom of heaven. Blessed are you when they revile and persecute you, and say all kinds of evil against you falsely for My sake. Rejoice and be exceedingly glad, for great is your reward in heaven, for so they persecuted the prophets who were before you....You have heard that it was said, 'You shall love your neighbor and hate your enemy.' But I say to you, love your enemies, bless those who curse you, do good to those who hate you, and pray for those who spitefully use you and persecute you, that you may be sons of your Father in heaven; for He makes His sun rise on the evil and on the good, and sends rain on the just and on the unjust."* Matthew 5:9-12, 43-45

I hope you choose to receive Jesus, let His love and truth draw you into His band of believers and become a shining light to our dark world as His love shines through you.

Questions for Chapter 3

1. What is the basis – the foundational truth – which supports both the sanctity of life and the sanctity of marriage?

2. What does distorted diversity produce?

3. Why is so-called "gay marriage" not gay, not marriage, and not diversity?

4. How do we know that homosexuality is not "immutable" (unchangeable)?

5. What is the ultimate confusion? Why?

6. What is at the core of rebellion against God?

7. What does the command, "You shall not covet," have to do with the issue of homosexuality?

8. Can you name Biblical principles that are flagrantly violated in so-called "Gay Pride Parades?"

9. Are human beings basically good by nature? Why or why not?

10. Can we actually have victory over our own struggles and temptations? How?

CHAPTER 4:

Passionate for Purity

Why Compromise the Purity Principal by Complying with Corrupt Culture?

I want to begin this chapter by sharing with you a copy of a letter I wrote to Shawn McMullen, editor of *The Lookout* magazine dated February 27, 2012.

Dear Shawn,

I'm writing in response to your February 19 issue, *Christians and Culture*. Your Secret Service Saturday is a great idea! I believe the articles "First Century Culture Shapers" and "Hold It Out" both have excellent input, but the article in between them, "Listening with Open Ears" I believe is dangerously flawed in its advice. Will you pass on my letter to Nicole R. Pramik? Will you consider publishing it as an open letter to her and the editor?

Dear Nicole,

As I consider your article "Listening with Open Ears", I want to express full agreement with your first sentence: "While Christians are called to be different from the world, we have to be familiar with the culture we live in if we want to make an impact for Christ." However, your second sentence I believe is problematic. You wrote: "We should strive to be as aware of our culture as we are of Scripture so we can communicate Christ's truth in a way people can understand." Are you sure this advice is true and accurate according to the Word of God – especially in the specific way you are recommending to become "aware of our culture"? **The Word of God says,** *"Test everything. Hold on to the good."* 1 Thessalonians 5:21. Are you willing to test your advice?

1. **What about the test of target audience?** Were you intending this advice for seasoned veterans of cultural warfare whose minds are saturated with Scripture – or to every Christian, including the wobbly-legged new believer who is saturated already with this ungodly culture but almost totally ignorant of Scripture? Since you make no distinction in your article, it must be intended for all Christians. I believe this shows a severe lack of discernment. A fire chief doesn't send an untrained recruit into a highly dangerous situation without strong guidance and along with a seasoned veteran. Teenage readers in Christian families may already be seeking ways to convince their parents to let them compromise with their culture by watching MTV – so they can "relate" to their peers. Now they can listen to Madonna, "Lady" Gaga and Eminem and tell their parents they are doing "research" while saturating their minds and hearts with the filth of this world.

I am now a seasoned veteran – from engaging the hippy culture and the university students in Eugene, Oregon, from 1966-70, when I was a young preacher, to speaking at "Man and the Christian Worldview" symposiums and conferences in Ukraine where the minority of us as Christians were facing Marxist/atheist scientists and professors, plus some postmodern and new age practitioners. We were able to engage them by speaking truth in love and building bridges of friendship. Although some got angry, others made significant changes. However, even as a seasoned veteran, I do not intend to follow your advice. Why not? Because I know my own weakness and vulnerability. I did not grow up in a Christian home and I learned to swear by the time I could walk and talk. My biggest battle when I gave my life to Jesus at age 12 was to allow the Holy Spirit to purify my filthy mind and foul mouth. It is still an ongoing process after all of these years and sometimes I still have mental flashbacks. Why should I pay our corrupt culture to reprogram my mind and mouth with filth under the guise of "research"? A few years ago, after Dan Brown's book, *The DaVinci Code* had been made into a movie, I scanned the book as an apologetics research project. His concepts are so perverted and vile that I felt like I had just gone swimming in a sewer. I never intend to read another Dan Brown book unless he is truly converted. I can testify that it is possible (and necessary) to engage our wicked culture without swimming in their sewer.

2. **What about the test of considering the downward pull of human nature?** In light of this, I do believe your advice is naïve and ignores the Biblical teaching about how corrupt our human nature really is. Jeremiah wrote by inspiration, *"The heart of man is deceitful above all other things and desperately wicked."* Jeremiah 17:9. Paul by inspiration describes the battle with the old nature vividly in Romans chapter 7 – after describing radical conversion in chapter 6 and before describing triumphant victory in chapter 8. Here is his description in verses 13-20: *"Did that which is good, then, become death to me? By no means! But in order that sin might be recognized as sin, it produced death in me through what was good, so that through the commandment sin might become utterly sinful. We know that the law is spiritual; but I am unspiritual, sold as a slave to sin. I do not understand what I do. For what I want to do I do not do, but what I hate I do. And if I do what I do not want to do, I agree that the law is good. As it is, it is no longer I myself who do it, but it is sin living in me. I know that nothing good*

lives in me, that is, in my sinful nature. For I have the desire to do what is good, but I cannot carry it out. For what I do is not the good I want to do; no the evil I do not want to do - this I keep on doing. Now if I do what I do not want to do, it is no longer I who do it, but it is sin living in me that does it."

3. **What about the test of considering many strong warnings in Scripture to be very, very cautious?** I believe that your article not only ignores the severe battle between the flesh and the spirit, but also the strong warnings given to us in the Word of God. Most modern movies contain pornography and often graphic, excessive violence. Do I need to dive into the sewer to know that it stinks, or to find some delicious morsel that accidently got flushed down the toilet? Here are some of the warnings and admonitions of Scripture: *"I made a covenant with my eyes not to look lustfully at a girl"* Job 31:1. *"For these commands are a lamp, this teaching is a light, and the corrections of discipline are the way to life, keeping you from the immoral woman, from the smooth tongue of the wayward wife. Do not lust in your heart after her beauty or let her captivate you with her eyes, for the prostitute reduces you to a loaf of bread, and the adulteress preys upon your very life. Can a man scoop fire into his lap without his clothes being burned?"* Proverbs 6:23-27. *"Do not be misled. Bad company corrupts good character."* 1 Corinthians 15:33. Lady Gaga? Eminem? *"Blessed are the pure in heart, for they shall see God"* Matthew 5:8. *"See to it that no one takes you captive through hollow and deceptive philosophy, which depends on human tradition and the basic principles of this world rather than on Christ."* Colossians 2:8. *"Therefore, dear friends, since you already know this, be on your guard so that you may not be carried away by the error of lawless men and fall from your secure position."* 2 Peter 3:17. *"Finally, brothers, whatever is true, whatever is noble, whatever is right, whatever is pure, whatever is lovely, whatever is admirable – if anything is excellent or praiseworthy – think about such things."* Philippians 4:8.

Can I watch the pornography in most movies and listen to the verbal filth in many of the popular songs and remain pure in heart? Can

I concentrate on what is pure and lovely while listening to Eminem or Madonna - even if I'm searching for what is good? Here is another pertinent warning: *"Therefore let him who thinks he stands take heed lest he fall."* 1 Corinthians 10:12.

I heard a story (on Family Life Today, I believe) about a father whose teenagers were pressing him to allow them to go see a movie their friends told them was great. They admitted to him that it had a few bad parts but told him how great was the theme and other redeeming characteristics they had heard about. He told them he would think it over and pray about it.

Soon he presented them with a plate of chocolate chip cookies he had made for them and told them of the high-quality ingredients he used – "However, along with the chocolate chips I also sprinkled in a few rabbit droppings," he told them. Their smiles changed to shocked expressions and they refused to eat the cookies. "If you won't eat my cookies – you don't go to the movie," he told them. I believe he was one wise father – don't you? Are we as concerned about moral and spiritual filth as we are about physical filth?

Randy Alcorn wrote a pertinent article entitled "The Radical Path to Purity" which was adapted from his powerful little book, *The Purity Principle.* Here is how he began the article.

"Suppose I said, 'There's a great-looking girl down the street. Let's go look through her window and watch her undress, then pose for us naked, from the waist up. Then this girl and her boyfriend will get in a car and have sex – let's listen and watch the windows steam up!'

You'd be shocked. You'd think, *What a pervert!*

But suppose instead I said, 'Hey, come on over. Let's watch *Titanic.*'

Christians recommend this movie, church youth groups view it together, and many have shown it in their homes. Yet the movie contains precisely the scenes I described.

So, as our young men lust after bare breasts on the screen, our young women are trained in how to get a man's attention.

How does something shocking and shameful somehow become acceptable because we watch it through a television instead of a window?

In terms of the lasting effects on our minds and morals, what's the difference?

Yet many think, *Titanic*? Wonderful! It wasn't even rated R!

Every day Christians across the country, including many church leaders, watch people undress through the window of television. We peek on people committing fornication and adultery, which our God calls an abomination.

We've become voyeurs, Peeping Toms, entertained by sin.

Normalizing evil

The enemy's strategy is to normalize evil. Consider young people struggling with homosexual temptation. How does it affect them when they watch popular television dramas where homosexual partners live together in apparent normality?

Parents who wouldn't dream of letting a dirty-minded adult baby-sit their children do it every time they let their kids surf the channels. Not only we, but our children become desensitized to immorality. Why are we surprised when our son gets a girl pregnant if we've allowed him to watch hundreds of immoral acts and hear thousands of jokes with sexual innuendos?...

But it's just one little sex scene.

Suppose I offered you a cookie, saying, "A few mouse droppings fell in the batter, but for the most part it's a great cookie – you won't even notice."

'To fear the LORD is to hate evil' (Proverbs 8:13). When we're being entertained by evil, how can we hate it? How can we

be pure when we amuse ourselves with impurity?" (Used by permission from Randy Alcorn.)

How Would You Rescue Someone from Quicksand?

As I see it, giving the advice to "Listen with Open Ears" to music with foul lyrics and watch movies with filthy pornography to someone with my background is like telling a former alcoholic to listen for good messages in beer commercials and concentrate his witnessing in the liquor stores and bars. He may reach someone, but he is putting himself on very shaky ground. If you are wearing white gloves to work in the garden, are you more likely to see muddy gloves or glovey mud?

For years I've heard the cliché about someone being "too heavenly minded to be of any earthly use", but strangely enough I've rarely met anyone like that. However, I've met, seen and read about hundreds of Christians who were too worldly minded to be of any heavenly use. If you want to rescue someone from the quicksand – throw him a rope. Don't jump into it with him to try to lift him out.

It is a known fact that pornography addiction is epidemic, and good sources of information like Family Life Today and Focus on the Family have documented that a very high percentage of church leaders are secretly pornography addicts. Yet you recommend listening with open ears and watching with open eyes to pornography laced music and movies! Is that going to help spread "the aroma of Christ" in our sick world? Already, about 80% of teens drop out of youth groups and church. Many never return. How do you think your advice is going to affect a group that is already so vulnerable?

Dear Nicole, please reconsider and rewrite your article. As it now stands, I believe it is a dangerous delusion that can produce perilous consequences.

"May the God of hope fill you with all joy and peace as you trust in Him, so that you may overflow with hope by the power of the Holy Spirit." Romans 15:13

Yours & His, Rick Deighton

Pornography is Pervasive and Progressive – Perverted and Pernicious

What is the attraction of pornography? It is appealing to our baser nature. All of us are born with that perverted nature from our fallen parents (all the way back to Eden), which is attracted to evil, like iron to a magnet. The combination of the natural, God-given attraction of male to female and female to male coupled with the innate curiosity of childhood, produces an instant attraction to images of nude humans, especially of the opposite sex. Discipline is essential to discipleship! We must learn to resist, overcome, and control our natural inclinations by the power of the Word and the Spirit, or we will be sucked into all manner of pernicious perversions. Pornography is probably the most pervasive. The problem of pornography addiction, even among Christian leaders, is pitiful and pathetic. The power of Jesus can break this – and is giving victory. You can get help through many ministries including Family Life Today, Family Talk, Focus on the Family, and AFA. Every one of these can help you get a filter for your computer. Satan is out to get you, and you are allowing him to play you for a fool if you don't get a filter. Pornography is like quicksand – it's a lot easier to get into it than to get out!

My earliest exposure to pornography that I remember was a pinup picture prominently portrayed in a mechanic shop. The problem now is that I can see such pinup pictures prominently portrayed on magazine racks in grocery stores near checkout stands, which are practically as pornographic as the Playboy centerfolds of the 1950s.

My next exposure that I remember was in the 6th grade when another boy and I found a portion of a pornographic magazine on or near the playground. When our teacher found us behind the building staring at the pictures, she threw a fit! I distinctly remember that she was not pleased with our covert activity. Good! I needed that! It's possible that she could have handled the problem better, but the fact is, she made her point in a way that we didn't forget! Why are more women not outraged now? Female flesh is being flagrantly flaunted before our male eyes, often by those females themselves. I realize that "modest apparel" is no longer easy to find for females, but conscientious Christians will not capitulate to corrupt culture! Where there is a will, there is a way.

By the way, when the two of us 6th graders got caught red handed, we did not even come up with a clever excuse like, "We want to become doctors, so we are doing scientific research in human anatomy." I doubt if she would have swallowed that lie anyway. We stood there as flat-footed, foolish, silent sinners before her righteous wrath. I thank God for her now.

What about Classic Art?

When Michelangelo was a young artist and began painting nude pictures, his teacher asked him why he was doing that. He replied that he wanted to paint people as God sees us. His teacher wisely replied, **"Michelangelo, you are not God!"**

Passion for Perversity

Richard Dawkins, one of the most blatant and brazen atheists in the world, promotes the idea, "There is no God –so go ahead and have fun!" Isn't this revealing of his true motive? Could it be that his concept of fun is warped and perverted? Paul spoke of false teachers as *"men of corrupt minds"* 2 Timothy 3:8, and also pointed out *"To the pure all things are pure, but to those who are defiled and unbelieving nothing is pure; but even their mind and conscience are defiled"* Titus 1:15.

Julian Huxley was perhaps even more brazen in his reply as to why Darwin's book, *The Origin of Species,* was so readily accepted and quickly became so widely popular. He answered the interviewer, "I suppose the reason we leapt at 'The Origin' is that we didn't like the idea of God interfering with our sexual mores." **How revealing!** How honest that he did not say, "because evolution is a fact!" as he asserted in the introduction he wrote for the centennial edition of *The Origin of Species.* R.C. Sproul has candidly observed and pointed out that when Bertrand Russell penned his infamous book, *Why I Am Not a Christian,* he neglected to mention his most basic reason – his adulterous escapades. R.C. also quipped that Russell's printed reasons are so easy to answer and refute. Bertrand Russell lived in a different era and was not so flippant and blatant about his true motives. **The underlying motive for adopting evolutionism is sex – not science!**

In considering this sub-heading of "Passion for Perversity" I don't want to pass up the perverse plans, program, and purpose of Planned Parenthood. As is true with other propaganda, such as the twisted use of the formerly good, joyous word "gay" as a synonym for homosexuality, likewise the term "Planned Parenthood" is a propaganda term for planned pushing of immoral sex as a means of harvesting multiple millions of dollars in abortions – both from the victims of their slaughter houses and from all of us as American taxpayers. The Planned Parenthood abortion mills are the most unregulated clinics in America – and more evidence keeps stacking up that they are also the most unsanitary. The "back alley" abortions are now gone, but the unsanitary, filthy butcher shop conditions prevail. I pray that the current lawsuits against Planned Parenthood will prevail and bring down this gigantic perpetrator of filth and murder. I want to share with you a brief article from *Citizen Magazine* that may shock you. However, if you know a little bit about Margaret Sanger, the founder (root) of Planned Parenthood, then you won't be surprised with the fruit of her efforts. "Jezebel" would be too polite of a label for the real Margaret Sanger. Now consider this brief look at . . .

"The Real Planned Parenthood"

"Planned Parenthood thinks there's something wrong with the sexual morals of young people: These kids today are just too ... conservative.

You read that right. On PP's Facebook page for teens, they've linked to an MTV video calling on kids to quit being judgmental toward promiscuity – or, as the video puts it, to 'stop the slut-shaming.'

'A lot of people define 'slut' as someone who has too much sex or too many partners,' says the speaker, a purported 'sexpert' named Francisco. 'But according to who? The slut fairy?'

Francisco doesn't want to banish the offending term, however. Just the opposite. He tells the kids that 'slut' should be used 'in a positive way' to describe 'a woman who is confident in her sexuality,' He says 'there's a little bit of slut in all of us ... So embrace it! 'Slut' should only be used for good.'

Well now. When PP talks to parents, they swear they're not encouraging teen sex, merely trying to control its consequences. When they talk to kids, they talk ... well, like this.

Next time someone asks you why Planned Parenthood shouldn't be talking to our kids in school, just tell 'em about Francisco. That should be all they'll need to hear." ("Citizen Magazine", December 2012. Used by permission.)

The real Planned Parenthood is planned perversity!

Samson

A He Man with a She Problem!

Was Samson the strongest man who ever lived, or the weakest? That depends on whether we are considering his muscles or his morals. He had a wholesome home and healthy heritage. God granted him supernatural, superior strength to serve his nation of suppressed servants as deliverer and judge, but he foolishly and frivolously squandered his physical potency on pagan Philistine fillies. One of his loose lovers was also a liberal liar who loved money more than muscles. Certainly, Samson's safety was not her primary priority. Her treacherous tears tricked Samson into telling her the truth about the source of his superior strength. She cuddled him, then coerced him into getting clipped, captured, and conquered. His physical power fell prey to the trap of Philistine female flesh and flirtation because he was a weak-willed wimp when it came to spiritual strength.

Isn't it interesting that the first recorded words of Samson are, "I saw a woman – get her for me!"? When the Philistine warriors captured him, they burned out his eyes with a hot poker so he could never again see a woman. (Friend, it is wise for us to keep our eyes on Jesus, don't you think?) After binding him and blinding him, they tied him to a millstone to use him for grinding grain. Let's remember that silly Samson suffered subjugation because he squandered his supernatural strength on sinful satisfaction. Let's never forget that sin binds, sin blinds, and sin grinds!

Sin will lead you farther than you intended to go away.

Sin will keep you longer than you intended to stay.

Sin will cost you more than you ever intended to pay!

God allowed devious, deceitful Delilah to bring sinful Samson down. He played with fire and got burned! The good news is that a story is not over till it's over! There is a strong suggestion that Samson submitted to the Savior and repented. When he cried out to God at the Philistine festival, the Almighty renewed Samson's strength and restored his resolve. In his death, Samson conquered more pagan Philistines than he did in his life.

Now let's take a look at some insightful excerpts from Ravi Zacharias' article, "Evicting the Sacred":

Evicting the Sacred from Society

"… I am a Christian. When I came to America decades ago, I was thrilled to see Christmas celebrated and the reason for the season so obvious: the birth of Jesus Christ. Did I assume that every American was thus a Christian? Certainly not. But I expected the charitable heart of even the dissenter to allow that which has been practiced in this country historically and traditionally to continue.

But alas, it is not so. In Thailand and Indonesia Christmas carols are sung in shopping centers and Christmas trees adorn airports. But in America the anti-Christian bias of silly advertisements like Bloomingdales' 'Merry, Happy, Love, Peace' reflect ideas firmly planted in midair and proclaim no reason for the season.

Who is offended by a public celebration of Christmas? The anti-Christian secularist who lives under the illusion that values are cradled in a vacuum. Peace and love for what? What do these terms really mean? Are they self-evident? Not by any means.

America may not be a Christian nation per-se, but only the Judeo-Christian worldview could have framed such a nation's ideas and values: 'All men are created equal, that they are endowed by their Creator with certain unalienable Rights.' No other religion or secular assumption can affirm such a statement except the Judeo-Christian worldview. But today that very worldview, on which our systems of government and law are based, is expelled from the marketplace.

Democracies that are unhinged from all sacred moorings ultimately sink under the brute weight of conflicting egos. Freedom is destroyed not just by its retraction, but more often by its abuse.

Is it not odd that whenever it has power, liberalism is anything but liberal, both in the area of religion and politics? We now have something called 'spirituality' because people don't like the word 'religion.' What does spirituality mean? It means you may believe anything you wish to believe but regarding ultimate things, 'No absolutes, please.' **The relativism and spirituality with which our society lives have one thing in common: they are both sophisticated ways of self-worship.**

It is not accidental that even as Christian values have been jettisoned, the world is economically and morally on the verge of bankruptcy. Oh, but Jesus' Name still surfaces in the West. Maybe more often than any other name. Why? Because profanity still reigns. Oh yes, and God still figures in our philosophy: even when 'Mother Earth' quakes and thousands die, we still blame 'Father God.' The banishment of Christmas may be the anti-theists' great longing. But they still want the gifts of Christmas – love, joy, peace, and reason. **Malcolm Muggeridge once opined that we have educated ourselves into imbecility.**

What are we celebrating at Christmas? What is the message of Christmas? It is the birth of the One Who promised peace, joy, and love. Try as we will, we cannot realize such values without acknowledging the point of reference for these absolutes: the very person of God and His gift to us of a changed heart and will. **That message needs to be heard around our world that is reeling with problems and rife with hate. For we have proven we are not fit to be God.**

G.K. Chesterton was right: **'The problem with Christianity is not that it has been tried and found wanting, but that it has been found difficult and left untried.'**

Some years ago, I walked into the Forbidden City in Beijing. It was a cold and grey January. I paused as I saw deep inside its walls a shop with the banner still fluttering, 'Merry Christmas.' That which was happily displayed in the Forbidden City is now all but forbidden in our cities. A Chinese professor once remarked to me, 'You Christians need to thank God for Communism, because we left the souls of our people empty, making room for the gospel.' Maybe someday we will thank the rabid secularists as well, when Merry Christmas will no longer be forbidden in our cities. **Exhausted and disappointed in self-worship, we may turn to God again and hear His story afresh."** – Dr. Ravi Zacharias is the president and CEO of Ravi Zacharias International Ministries (rzim.org), a speaker and author of Why Jesus? Rediscovering His Truth in an Age of the Mass marketed Spirituality. ("Samaritan Ministries", December 2012, pp. 1, 7. Used by permission.)

Secularism is bias against the sacred.

Know Thyself

I want to pick up and expand on Ravi's sentence, *"Exhausted and disappointed in self-worship, we may turn to God again and hear His story afresh."*

Was it Socrates or Plato who wrote, "Know thyself!"? Do you realize that this is part of the foolish pagan philosophy which contradicts the truth revealed to us by Almighty God? Are you a committed Christian? A semi-committed Christian? If so, why follow the pagan advice to "Know thyself "? Do you realize that you can waste hours, days, months, even years seeking to find yourself? If you do accomplish that goal of "finding yourself', what will you find? You will find a fool who has been wasting much time with such a futile pursuit! Suddenly you will realize that it was a foolish, self-centered pursuit impossible to attain because the only one who knows your heart is God Himself. *"The heart is deceitful above all things, And desperately wicked; Who can know it? I, the LORD, search the heart, I test the mind, Even to give every man according to his ways, According to the fruit of his doings."* Jeremiah 17:9-10. Your search to know yourself has likely degenerated into searching for love and meaning in all the wrong places – power, prestige, and pleasure (sexual immorality). Wouldn't it be so much wiser to follow the example of the apostle Paul who, even years after his dramatic conversion, made it his goal and passion to know Christ? Could this be the reason he became the second most influential man in history? (Jesus is the first – no doubt about it!) *"But what things were gain to me, these I have counted loss for Christ. Yet indeed I also count all things loss for the excellence of the knowledge of Christ Jesus my Lord, for whom I have suffered the loss of all things, and count them as rubbish, that I may gain Christ and be found in Him, not having my own righteousness, which is from the law, but that which is through faith in Christ, the righteousness which is from God by faith; that I may know Him and the power of His resurrection, and the fellowship of His sufferings, being conformed to His death, if, by any means, I may attain to the resurrection from the dead. Not that I have already attained, or am already perfected; but I press on, that I may lay hold of that for which Christ Jesus has also laid hold of me. Brethren, I do not count myself to have apprehended; but one thing I do, forgetting those things which are behind and reaching forward to those things which are ahead. I press toward the goal for the prize of the upward call of God in Christ Jesus. Therefore let us, as many as are mature, have this mind; and if in anything you think otherwise, God will reveal even this to you."* Philippians 3:7-15.

The Beautiful and the Ugly, The Exciting and the Boring

There is nothing so beautiful as that which is good. There is nothing so ugly and boring as that which is evil.

Satan uses fiction and our vivid imaginations to turn that around. He makes evil look exciting, fascinating, intriguing, and attractive. Revival preacher, Archie Word, warned us not to be captivated by the liquor ads with beautiful women dressed in black velvet. Look under the billboard to see the drunk wallowing in his own vomit for the true picture. Sin has pleasure for a season – then comes the bitter payoff. **Yes, there will be payday someday!**

Christ candidly warns us of trials and hardship when we take up our cross to follow Him, but the rewards are out of this world!

Warped or Wonderful?

Satan appeals to the imagination by making evil appear intriguing, exciting, and fun. He also lies to us that following Christ is boring. The opposite is true! **Would you like to join me in the exciting adventure of following Jesus?** *"You therefore, my son, be strong in the grace that is in Christ Jesus. And the things that you have heard from me among many witnesses, commit these to faithful men who will be able to teach others also. You therefore must endure hardship as a good soldier of Jesus Christ. No one engaged in warfare entangles himself with the*

affairs of this life, that he may please him who enlisted him as a soldier."
2 Timothy 2:1-4

It is Likely That a Liberal Has More Confidence in His Dog than in Our God – or Our Kids!

Recently on a "Breakpoint" radio program one of the speakers told that when they were promoting abstinence education instead of the Planned Parenthood Program of so-called "comprehensive sex education" (which is **definitely** not comprehensive because they spurn and mock abstinence education) a listener responded by saying that the kids need condom education because they are going to do it anyway. "To think otherwise is foolish," he told them. Obviously the one who responded has absorbed and adopted the liberal lie that the kids are going to follow their natural urges and fornicate no matter what we say or do to prevent it. Why am I so brazen as to label this a "liberal lie"? Because it is, that's why!

1. Are you aware that Uganda adopted abstinence education to stem the tide of death by AIDS – and in just a few years have been hugely successful? If I remember correctly, they lowered the number of AIDS cases by somewhere between 60% to 80%! Yet to our shame as a nation our Former Secretary of State, Hillary Clinton, went to Uganda and threatened to withdraw our financial support unless they switch to the Planned Parenthood program of promiscuous perversion. How outrageous!

2. Are you aware that abstinence only education courses here in the US have been amazingly successful in lowering unwed pregnancies, abortions, and sexually transmitted diseases?

3. Are you aware of the fact that some liberals own house-trained dogs? Isn't that amazing? **These liberals have confidence that they can train their dogs to control their natural urges – yet strongly declare that we cannot train our kids to control their natural urges!** They have more confidence in their dogs than

their kids – and our kids! **Are you outraged yet? If not, why not?**

By the way, who is it who is being foolish?

What is the Difference between Legalism and Liberalism?

Legalism specializes in condemning.

Liberalism specializes in condoning.

Jesus specializes in forgiving and then empowering.

When the scribes and the Pharisees brought in to Jesus an adulteress in an attempt to trap Him, they found themselves caught in their own trap. At this point in this captivating account, "Jesus stood up and said to her, 'Woman, where are they? Has no one condemned you?' She said, 'No one, Lord.' And Jesus said, 'Neither do I condemn you; go, and from now on sin no more.'" John 8:10-11 (ESV)

The woman was already condemned by the Law of God, but Jesus skillfully and wisely turned the trap around to close on the hypocrites to see that they were also under the hammer of the law of God while seeking to use this sinful, but helpless woman as their bait to trap and condemn Jesus.

Have you ever wondered what Jesus wrote in the sand? The text doesn't say – but the context indicates to me that the first time He knelt and wrote it probably read, "Where is the man?" They had already told Him that this woman was caught in the act, so the logical question would be, "Where is the man?" Maybe it was one of them! The next time He knelt to write, I think He wrote the name of the adulteress that the oldest man among had been with – then turned and looked him in the eye. After him, the next oldest. The text says: "But when they heard it, they went away one by one, beginning with the older ones, and Jesus was left alone with the woman standing before him." John 8:9 (ESV)

Jesus came to seek and to save the lost - and He did so without becoming either a legalist or a liberal. Let's go and do likewise! (By the way, He was the one who sought them first – before they were seeking Him – as with the woman at the well.)

Are we Setting the Right Example?

If we are going to train our children to control their sexual urges, to respect their own bodies and the bodies of those of the opposite sex as amazing creations of Almighty God, and to save their intimate expressions of affection for the one and only person he or she marries, then we must set the right kind of example.

Hot Clothes and Burning Feet
(The Path of Destruction and How to Avoid It)

"For the commandment is a lamp, and the law a light; reproofs of instruction are the way of life, to keep you from the evil woman, from the flattering tongue of a seductress. Do not lust after her beauty in your heart, nor let her allure you with her eyelids. For by means of a harlot a man is reduced to a crust of bread; and an adulteress will prey upon his precious life. **Can a man take fire to his bosom, and his clothes not be burned? Can one walk on hot coals, and his feet not be seared?** *So is he who goes in to his neighbor's wife; whoever touches her shall not be innocent. People do not despise a thief if he steals to satisfy himself when he is starving. Yet when he is found, he must restore sevenfold; he may have to give up all the substance of his house. Whoever commits adultery with a woman lacks understanding; he who does so destroys his own soul. ... And there a woman met him, with the attire of a harlot, and a crafty heart. ... Do not let your heart turn aside to her ways, do not stray into her paths; for she has cast down many wounded, and all who were slain by her were strong men. Her house is the way to hell, descending to the chambers of death."* Proverbs 6:23-32; 7:10, 25-27

"You, therefore, who teach another, do you not teach yourself? You

who preach that a man should not steal, do you steal? You who say, "Do not commit adultery," do you commit adultery?" Romans 2:21-22

Abstain

"Beloved, I urge you as sojourners and exiles to abstain from the passions of the flesh, which wage war against your soul. Keep your conduct among the Gentiles honorable, so that when they speak against you as evildoers, they may see your good deeds and glorify God on the day of visitation.... For this is the will of God, that by doing good you should put to silence the ignorance of foolish people. Live as people who are free, not using your freedom as a cover-up for evil, but living as servants of God. ... For what credit is it if, when you sin and are beaten for it, you endure? But if when you do good and suffer for it you endure, this is a gracious thing in the sight of God. For to this you have been called, because Christ also suffered for you, leaving you an example, so that you might follow in his steps. He committed no sin, neither was deceit found in his mouth. When he was reviled, he did not revile in return; when he suffered, he did not threaten, but continued entrusting himself to him who judges justly. He himself bore our sins in his body on the tree, that we might die to sin and live to righteousness. By his wounds you have been healed." 1 Peter 2:11-12; 2:15-16, 20-24 (ESV)

"So live that you would not be afraid to sell the family parrot to the town gossip!" ~Will Rogers

If I listen to things that are ungodly;
If I look at things that are ungodly;
If I run with people that are ungodly. . .

then I am sowing to the flesh and I will reap destruction – not only in my life, but also in my children's lives! **So remember – and never forget:** *"No temptation has overtaken you except such as is common to man; but **God is faithful, who will not allow you to be tempted beyond what you are able,** but with the temptation will also make the*

*way of escape, that you may be able to bear it. . . **Therefore, whether you eat or drink, or whatever you do, do all to the glory of God.***"
1 Corinthians 10:13, 31.

Our Potent, Pertinent, Powerful Purity Principle

Here are powerful excerpts from the most potent power for purity in this world –the Word of God inspired by the Spirit of God. The Psalmist wrote, "*How can a young man cleanse his way? By taking heed according to Your word. With my whole heart I have sought You; oh, let me not wander from Your commandments! Your word I have hidden in my heart, that I might not sin against You.*" Psalm 119:9-11

Actually, I really need to clarify more completely that at the time the Psalmist wrote Psalm 119:11, the most potent power for purity was the Word of God hidden in the heart, but now we who are Christians have even far more potent power – the Holy Spirit Himself dwelling in our hearts to empower us to obey His Word hidden in our hearts. That's amazing! That's liberating! That's victorious!

What is Legitimate Pleasure?
(My notes from a radio message by Ravi Zacharias)

1. Any pleasure that refreshes without distracting you from, diminishing or destroying your final goal in life is a legitimate pleasure.

2. Any pleasure that jeopardizes the wellbeing of others is an illegitimate pleasure!

3. Any pleasure, however good, if not kept in balance will destroy appetite. All pleasures must be kept in balance with all of life. A time for everything.

Conclusion

1. All pleasure must be bought at the price of pain. Legitimate pleasure – you pay first.

2. Meaninglessness does not come from being weary of pain; meaninglessness comes from being weary of pleasure.

3. The closer you get to pure pleasures, the closer you get to the heart of God. The closer you get to impure pleasure the farther you get from God.

4. What does your heart long for? Intimacy that touches both body and soul. Communion!

Adoration of God is the greatest and highest expression of pleasure!

The Sign and Seal of the New Covenant

Do you realize what is the sign and seal of the New Covenant? Do you realize what the New Covenant actually is? On the Passover eve before He was crucified, Jesus instituted the New Covenant. *"And He took bread, gave thanks and broke it, and gave it to them, saying, 'This is My body which is given for you; do this in remembrance of Me.' Likewise He also took the cup after supper, saying, 'This cup is the new covenant in My blood, which is shed for you.'"* Luke 22:19-20.

So, what is the New Covenant (New Testament)? Note that it is not a book! I realize that we have printed copies of the New Covenant Scriptures with New Testament printed on the cover. In Jesus' own words we have the clarification that **the New Covenant is in His blood. It is a blood covenant relationship with God through the sacrifice of Jesus Christ.** We enter this covenant of grace by faith in His blood sacrifice for our sin when we repent and are baptized into Christ. The sign of the New Covenant is the cup containing fruit of the vine representing the blood of Jesus and the seal of our entrance into this New Covenant is the gift of the Holy Spirit. The Sabbath was the sign and seal of the Old Covenant between God and the nation of Israel. (Please see Exodus 31:12-18.) The Sabbath is not the sign and seal of the New Covenant.

Please carefully and prayerfully read these Scriptures:

*"Then Peter said to them, 'Repent, and let every one of you be baptized in the name of Jesus Christ for the remission of sins; and you shall receive **the gift of the Holy Spirit.** For the promise is to you and to your children, and to all who are afar off, as many as the Lord our God will call.'"* Acts 2:38-39.

*"There is therefore now no condemnation to those who are in Christ Jesus, who do not walk according to the flesh, but according to the Spirit. For the law of the Spirit of life in Christ Jesus has made me free from the law of sin and death . . . **But you are not in the flesh but in the Spirit, if indeed the Spirit of God dwells in you. Now if anyone does not have the Spirit of Christ, he is not His.** And if Christ is in you, the body is dead because of sin, but the Spirit is life because of righteousness. **But if the Spirit of Him who raised Jesus from the dead dwells in you, He who raised Christ from the dead will also give life to your mortal bodies through His Spirit who dwells in you."** Romans 8:1-2, 9-11.*

*"**Now He who establishes us with you in Christ and has anointed us is God, who also has sealed us and given us the Spirit in our hearts as a guarantee."** 2 Corinthians 1:21-22.*

*"Now He who has prepared us for this very thing is **God, who also has given us the Spirit as a guarantee.** So we are always confident, knowing that while we are at home in the body we are absent from the Lord. For we walk by faith, not by sight. We are confident, yes, well pleased rather to be absent from the body and to be present with the Lord."* 2 Corinthians 5:5-8.

*"In Him you also trusted, after you heard the word of truth, the gospel of your salvation; in whom also, **having believed, you were sealed with the Holy Spirit of promise,"** Ephesians 1:13.*

Live a life of Truth, Beauty, Victory and Purity!

If you truly want to live a life of truth, beauty, victory, and purity then keep your eyes on Jesus, your heart filled with the Holy Spirit, and your feet on the straight and narrow!

1. **Eyes** on Jesus

a. *"Therefore we also, since we are surrounded by so great a cloud of witnesses, let us lay aside every weight, and the sin which so easily ensnares us, and let us run with endurance the race that is set before us,* **looking unto Jesus, the author and finisher of our faith,** *who for the joy that was set before Him endured the cross, despising the shame, and has sat down at the right hand of the throne of God.* **For consider Him who endured such hostility from sinners against Himself, lest you become weary and discouraged in your souls."** Hebrews 12:1-3.

b. *"But we all, with unveiled face,* **beholding as in a mirror the glory of the Lord, are being transformed into the same image from glory to glory, just as by the Spirit of the Lord."** 2 Corinthians 3:18.

2. **Heart** Filled with the Holy Spirit

a. *"Therefore do not be unwise, but understand what the will of the Lord is. And do not be drunk with wine, in which is dissipation;* **but be filled with the Spirit,** *speaking to one another in psalms and hymns and spiritual songs, singing and making melody in your heart to the Lord, giving thanks always for all things to God the Father in the name of our Lord Jesus Christ, submitting to one another in the fear of God."* Ephesians 5:17-21.

b. *"But above all these things put on love, which is the bond of perfection. And let the peace of God rule in your hearts, to which also you were called in one body; and be thankful.* **Let the word of Christ dwell in you richly in all wisdom,** *teaching and admonishing one another in psalms and hymns and spiritual songs, singing with grace in your hearts to the Lord.* **And whatever you do in word or deed, do all in the name of the Lord Jesus, giving thanks to God the Father through Him."** Colossians 3:14-17.

3. **Feet** on the Straight and Narrow

"'Enter by the narrow gate; for wide is the gate and broad is the way that leads to destruction, and there are many who go in by it. Because narrow is the gate and difficult is the way which leads to life, and there are few who find it." Matthew 7:13-14.

Does God Have a Sense of Humor?

Many years ago, I walked into a small fast-food restaurant in Nampa, Idaho about mid-afternoon to order a hamburger. There were no other customers and only one employee – a beautiful young lady. She was both waitress and cook, so she came over to my table, took my order, and walked back over to the grill. Even though I was already a happily married man, her beauty caught my attention, and without thinking about what I was doing I was staring at her as she walked back over to the grill. Then I noticed the sign posted directly above the stove where she was standing – "Keep Your Eyes on Jesus!" Suddenly I diverted my eyes from her to Jesus and said, "Yes, Sir!" (Silent prayer.) Does God have a sense of humor? What do you think?

A Time to Flee!

In that case I didn't flee – I stayed and ate my sandwich I had ordered. However, I want to tell you about another incident that took place a few years later at a water park in Boise on a hot summer day. I supplied lighting for the water park business and went there to check needs. On my way in, I walked past an attractive young lady wearing a swimsuit she had outgrown. As I exited the building, she winked at me as I went by. The thought did occur to me that I should take her a tract and witness to her, but the Holy Spirit reminded me that there was a time to flee. I prayed, "Lord, please send a woman to witness to her. I'm getting out of here!" There is a time to fight – and there is a time to flee!

I hope you hide some of these portions of His Word in your heart.

"What shall we say then? Shall we continue in sin that grace may

*abound? Certainly not! How shall we who died to sin live any longer in it? Or do you not know that as many of us as were baptized into Christ Jesus were baptized into His death? Therefore we were buried with Him through baptism into death, that just as Christ was raised from the dead by the glory of the Father, even so we also should walk in newness of life. For if we have been united together in the likeness of His death, certainly we also shall be in the likeness of His resurrection, knowing this, that our old man was crucified with Him, that the body of sin might be done away with, that we should no longer be slaves of sin. For he who has died has been freed from sin. Now if we died with Christ, we believe that we shall also live with Him, knowing that Christ, having been raised from the dead, dies no more. Death no longer has dominion over Him. For the death that He died, He died to sin once for all; but the life that He lives, He lives to God. Likewise you also, reckon yourselves to be dead indeed to sin, but alive to God in Christ Jesus our Lord. Therefore do not let sin reign in your mortal body, that you should obey it in its lusts. And do not present your members as instruments of unrighteousness to sin, but present yourselves to God as being alive from the dead, and your members as instruments of righteousness to God. **For sin shall not have dominion over you, for you are not under law but under grace.***"
Romans 6:1-14.

It's not What you Know, It's Who you Know!

*"And we know that all things work together for good to those who love God, to those who are the called according to His purpose. For whom He foreknew, He also predestined to be conformed to the image of His Son, that He might be the firstborn among many brethren. Moreover whom He predestined, these He also called; whom He called, these He also justified; and whom He justified, these He also glorified... Yet in all **these things we are more than conquerors through Him who loved us.***"* Romans 8:28-30, 37.

Remember, it does **not** say that we **can be** more than conquerors – we **are** more than conquerors! Let's be who we are!

"Now the Lord is the Spirit; and where the Spirit of the Lord is, there is liberty. **But we all, with unveiled face, beholding as in a mirror the glory of the Lord, are being transformed into the same image from glory to glory, just as by the Spirit of the Lord."** 2 Corinthians 3:17-18.

"Brethren, join in following my example, and note those who so walk, as you have us for a pattern. For many walk, of whom I have told you often, and now tell you even weeping, that **they are the enemies of the cross of Christ: whose end is destruction, whose god is their belly, and whose glory is in their shame—who set their mind on earthly things.** *For our citizenship is in heaven, from which we also eagerly wait for the Savior, the Lord Jesus Christ, who will transform our lowly body that it may be conformed to His glorious body, according to the working by which He is able even to subdue all things to Himself."* Philippians 3:17-21.

Our part is not to glory in our shame, but to glory in our God! **"Rejoice in the Lord always. Again I will say, rejoice! Let your gentleness be known to all men. The Lord is at hand.** *Be anxious for nothing, but in everything by prayer and supplication, with thanksgiving, let your requests be made known to God; and the peace of God, which surpasses all understanding, will guard your hearts and minds through Christ Jesus. Finally, brethren, whatever things are true, whatever things are noble, whatever things are just, whatever things are pure, whatever things are lovely, whatever things are of good report, if there is any virtue and if there is anything praiseworthy— meditate on these things."* Philippians 4:4-8.

Let us not be ashamed to stand up and speak out for purity, truth, righteousness and the glory of God as Paul did. *"And since we have the same spirit of faith, according to what is written, 'I believed and therefore I spoke,' we also believe and therefore speak, knowing that He who raised up the Lord Jesus will also raise us up with Jesus, and will present us with you. For all things are for your sakes, that grace, having spread through the many, may cause thanksgiving to abound to the glory of God."* 2 Corinthians 4:13-15.

The Power of a Positive NO!

If you are going to protect your purity – and the purity of your potential partner for life – you need to set boundaries!

- Boundaries on where and when you meet.

- Boundaries on what you look at and listen to.

- Boundaries on how much time you spend together – especially alone.

- Boundaries on how late you will be together.

- Boundaries on where you spend time together.

- Boundaries on the companions you spend time with. Remember: *"Do not be deceived: 'Evil company corrupts good habits.'"* 1 Corinthians 15:33

- Boundaries on kissing each other.

- Boundaries on where and how you touch each other.

I have 2 pertinent examples for you:

1. Biblical courtship should and can be a wonderful season of life – with no regrets. Years ago when Jim Dietrich started dating Connie Strubhar, Gary and Sandra's youngest daughter, he told her that he would never kiss her until and unless he intended to ask her to marry him. Why? Because he did not want to stir up passions it was not time to fulfill, and he did not want to break her heart or his own if they realized that it would not be a wise option for them to marry. One evening when he brought her home she bounced into the house brimming with excitement she could not contain – "Mom! Dad! Jim kissed me!" They all understood what that meant. Gary and Sandra were almost as excited as Connie because they had observed what an honorable young man Jim was, and would be glad to see him as their son-in-law – the spiritual leader and provider for their daughter.

How many teenage girls do you think are excited to come home to their parents to share the joy of saying, "He kissed me"? This type of openness builds strong family relationships instead of suspicion, mistrust, and aggravations. It's a beautiful thing!

Jim and Connie have been married for many years, have a grown son and daughter who love the Lord, and they serve as mentors for other couples on building strong marriage and family relationships.

2. On the radio, I heard Paul Shepherd share an illustration about a couple who nearly lost control when they were alone watching a movie with the lights turned low. They had failed to set the boundaries where they should have, and she was the one who got so stirred up she started putting the move on him. (Men aren't always the aggressive ones when it comes to inappropriate touching.) Fortunately – by the grace of God – this young man knew the power of a positive NO! He understood they were in spiritual and moral danger. He stood up, turned up the lights and said to her, "If you ever touch me like that again, you won't see me again!" The couple is now married, so his bold action probably saved their relationship. It definitely saved them from the sin of fornication! If they had compromised their convictions to their passions they would have trespassed on private property without a license, and would have committed a sin against God, against each other, and against their own bodies. *"Do you not know that your bodies are members of Christ? Shall I then take the members of Christ and make them members of a harlot? Certainly not! Or do you not know that he who is joined to a harlot is one body with her? For 'the two,' He says, 'shall become one flesh.' But he who is joined to the Lord is one spirit with Him.* **Flee sexual immorality.** *Every sin that a man does is outside the body, but **he who commits sexual immorality sins against his own body. Or do you not know that your body is the temple of the Holy Spirit who is in you, whom you have from God, and you are not your own? For you were bought at a price; therefore glorify God in your body and in your spirit, which are God's.*"** 1 Corinthians 6:15-20

Often the guilt which ensues after an immoral compromise destroys the relationship. The antidote for this nagging guilt is the grace of God with His forgiveness through the blood of Jesus Christ.

Have you received this forgiveness? He will cast your sin into the sea of His forgetfulness to be remembered no more!

Learn the power of a positive NO! (Ladies, your NO may need to be accompanied with the power of a positive slap in the face!)

Taking a Stand

When you take a stand on a standard – someone may call you a legalist. That's not legalism! Be careful what you do with grace. *"For the grace of God that brings salvation has appeared to all men, **teaching us that, denying ungodliness and worldly lusts, we should live soberly, righteously, and godly in the present age, looking for the blessed hope and glorious appearing of our great God and Savior Jesus Christ,** who gave Himself for us, that He might redeem us from every lawless deed and purify for Himself His own special people, zealous for good works. Speak these things, exhort, and rebuke with all authority. Let no one despise you."* Titus 2:11-15.

"Because the sentence against an evil work is not executed speedily, therefore the heart of the sons of men is fully set in them to do evil." Ecclesiastes 8:11

Purity – Not Perversion is the Alternative Lifestyle!

Jesus said, *"**Blessed are the pure in heart, for they shall see God.**"* Matthew 5:8.

God Does Want Me to be Happy – Doesn't He?

This is a common question in our corrupt culture. It came to my attention again recently when a believer told me that a man used this loaded question to her when she told him that she believes homosexuality is wrong. He responded, "God does want me to be happy, doesn't He?" How should we answer this question? Why not ask the questioner a counter question – "What makes you happy?" Or ask, "What is your definition of happiness?" If sinful behavior is your definition of being happy, then the answer is, NO!

It is true that there is in sinful behavior a fleeting fulfillment – then come the devastating, deplorable, degrading, destructive consequences! It is Satan who wants you to be happy – for a season – then reap the miserable consequences of sin in this life for the long term and in eternity forever. God wants you to practice self-control now and be happy now, next week, next month, next year – and forever!

Those who search for significance, self-worth, and satisfaction through sexting or any other perversion of their sexuality may find fleeting fun in flirting and following physical passions, but they will ultimately reap the bitter consequences. *"Do not be deceived, God is not mocked; for whatever a man sows, that he will also reap. For he who sows to his flesh will of the flesh reap corruption, but he who sows to the Spirit will of the Spirit reap everlasting life."* Galatians 6:7-8.

Yes, God Does Want You To Be Happy! Here's How!

(Note: The word "blessed" literally means "happy or blissful")

THE JESUS MANIFESTO

"Then He opened His mouth and taught them, saying:
"Blessed are the poor in spirit,
For theirs is the kingdom of heaven.
Blessed are those who mourn,
For they shall be comforted.
Blessed are the meek,
For they shall inherit the earth.

Blessed are those who hunger and thirst for righteousness,
For they shall be filled.
Blessed are the merciful,
For they shall obtain mercy.
Blessed are the pure in heart,
For they shall see God.
Blessed are the peacemakers,

For they shall be called sons of God.
Blessed are those who are persecuted for righteousness' sake,
For theirs is the kingdom of heaven.

"Blessed are you when they revile and persecute you, and say all kinds of evil against you falsely for My sake. Rejoice and be exceedingly glad, for great is your reward in heaven, for so they persecuted the prophets who were before you." Matthew 5:2-12.

These wonderful words are from the Master Messenger's Superb Sermon spoken on the side of a mountain. I call this The Jesus Manifesto. What a strong contrast to the Humanist Manifesto! (Humanist is very different from humanitarian.) The Jesus Manifesto produces humanitarians who reach out to suffering humans. The Humanist Manifesto produces secular sectarians like the Freedom From Religion Foundation and the American Civil Liberties Union. They expend a huge amount of time, money, and energy fighting God and undermining Christian influences in our nation – but where are their humanitarian projects? They want to tear down crosses, rip "Under God" from our Pledge of Allegiance, and "In God we Trust" from our money, and knock Ten Commandment monuments out of public view. **Their focus is on tearing down – not building up! They spurn the purity principle and promote all manner of sexual immorality, deviation, and perversion.**

My friend, weigh carefully what worldview you choose to accept, live by, and promote. Look both at the roots and the fruits of the philosophy which will define your life and your destiny!

The Jesus Manifesto – known by multitudes as The Beatitudes - has been praised and promoted by statesmen and scholars as the greatest manifesto ever given, and The Sermon on the Mount in which Jesus delivered His Manifesto as the most powerful message ever delivered. The Humanist Manifestos (both 1933 and 1973 versions) are a couple of duds in comparison. Not only are they duds - they are devious, deadly and destructive.

The Proper Role of Family, Church, and State

Almighty God is the Creator and Master of family, church, and state. He designed each of these institutions carefully with a different role to play in an orderly society. Each is a minister (servant) for the Master – and answerable to Him.

The Bottom Line

"*Yet in all these things we are more than conquerors through Him who loved us.* *For I am persuaded that neither death nor life, nor angels nor principalities nor powers, nor things present nor things to come, nor height nor depth, nor any other created thing, shall be able to separate us from the love of God which is in Christ Jesus our Lord.*" Romans 8:37-39

"**For God has not given us a spirit of fear, but of power and of love and of a sound mind.**" 2 Timothy 1:7. Courage is not the absence of fear – it is the conquering of fear! You will not be inhibited by fear if you are inhabited by the Holy Spirit. **We are more than conquerors through Him who loved us.**

WE MUST BE COURTEOUS –
BUT WE WILL NOT BE QUIET!

Potent Prayer

Lord, please fill me with Your Spirit and put me in the right place at the right time with the right words to honor You. Please give me the courage to confront and the grace to be courteous in the midst of our corrupted culture.

As you pray, remember that there are basically three kinds of people:

1. Those who are afraid.

2. Those who don't know enough to be afraid (the naïve).

3. Those who choose to trust God and believe His promises.

Supplement

I highly recommend you read these two articles, both found in the December 2012 issue of *afaJournal:*

"The Morally Heroic and the Rescue of Culture," by Ed Vitagliano (pp. 20-21)

"Christians Respond to Cries for Freedom," by Teddy James (pp. 22-23)

Questions for Chapter 4

1. What three vitally important tests was Nicole Pramik overlooking in her article, "Listening with Open Ears"?

2. Do you believe that watching a movie like *Titanic* is wholesome entertainment for believers? Why or why not?

3. What is the underlying motive for adopting evolutionism (or other non-Christian worldviews and religions)?

4. What is the real Planned Parenthood?

5. Why is secularism intent on evicting the sacred from society?

6. Is the Greek philosophy, "Know thyself," a Biblical teaching and an aspect of true wisdom? Why or why not?

7. Why is it likely that a liberal has more confidence in his dog than in our God?

8. What is our potent, pertinent, powerful purity principle?

9. What three things can we do to live a life of truth, beauty, victory, and purity?

10. Does God most want us to be happy or holy? Does God's description of what it takes to be truly happy (joyous) different from most human expectations?

"Covenant Eyes" software with accountability partners is highly recommended by Dr. James and Ryan Dobson for recovery from Pornography addiction.

CHAPTER 5

Knowledge of the Truth

We are so thankful to have the knowledge of the truth through our access to the Word of God, and we are also very thankful for the generous and gracious manner in which Institute for Creation Research (ICR) has been helping our small, struggling Northwest Science Museum for over five years now. They send us a box of 40 to 50 copies of their outstanding magazine, *Acts & Facts*, each month and a box of their insightful devotional booklets, *Days of Praise*, each quarter so we can distribute them to share the truth of Biblical Christian worldview. Why do they do this? Probably because:

1. In early June 2014, I wrote to ICR asking if they had any left-over copies of the June issue of *Acts & Facts* (in which the lead article by Henry M. Morris III stressed the truth that Jesus Christ Is the Foundation)! I mentioned that our "Grand Opening" day for our Vision Center would be June 14. To our surprise, they sent us a box filled with May and June issues of *Acts & Facts*. Month by month they have continued this generous and gracious practice!

2. Obviously, they believe Jesus' statement that, **"It is more blessed to give than to receive."**

Now in honor of ICR and appreciation for their generous support of NWSM, I want to announce that ICR plans to open to the pubic their big, beautiful Discovery Center for Science and Earth History on September 2, 2019 in Dallas, Texas. (I'm looking forward to the opportunity to go see it myself, and I hope you get to as well!)

Also, I want to share with you the devotional thought in *Days of Praise* for Sunday, August 4, 2019 by Henry M. Morris III, entitled "Knowledge of the Truth."

> "For this is good and acceptable in the sight of God our Saviour; Who will have all men to be saved, and to come unto the knowledge of the truth." (1 Timothy 2:3-4)

> "The phrase 'the truth,' referring to a certain vital body of doctrine, is found often in the New Testament, and the text quoted above is one of the most important, indicating as it does that fully understanding 'the truth' is equivalent to being saved.

> "The theme of 'the truth' is especially emphasized in Paul's two letters to Timothy, the first reference being in our text. He next points out that, in his capacity as an apostle, he must 'speak the truth in Christ,' teaching 'in faith and verity' (same word as 'truth'----1 Timothy 2:7).

> "The church is called 'the pillar and ground of the truth' (3:15). An attitude of thanksgiving is proper for those who 'believe and know the truth' (4:3). On the other hand, those false teachers who teach with selfish motives are 'destitute of the truth' (6:5).

> "In the second epistle, Paul urges believers to be diligent in studying the Scriptures, because they constitute 'the word of truth' (2 Timothy 2:15). Then he warns of teachers 'who concerning the truth have erred,' teaching false doctrine and destroying the faith of some (v. 18). Those who are faithful teachers, however, are exhorted to help the unsaved come to 'repentance to the acknowledging of the truth' (v. 25).

> "Then, in his prophetic description of the humanist teachers of the last days, Paul says they will be 'ever learning, and never able to come to the knowledge of the truth' (3:7). This is because they

'resist the truth' and 'turn away their ears from the truth' (3:8; 4:5). Thus, 'the truth' always emphasizes its vital importance in salvation and the Christian life. Most of all, the **Lord Jesus said; 'I am . . . the truth'** (John 14:6). HMM (Used by permission.)

Are you tired of the devolving of our formerly great American culture (based on Biblical Christian principles) deeper and deeper into immorality, impurity, cruelty and craziness? Tired of lawsuits to take down crosses, ban prayers, eliminate, "under God," from our pledge and destroy, "In God we Trust," as our national motto? Tired of crazy laws that allow a "trans" man to participate in women's sports, that protect any confused man who claims he feels he's a woman to enter girls' bathrooms and shower stalls, permit the bodies of unborn babies to be cut in pieces and ripped from their mothers' wombs, coddle brazen obscenity and flagrant pornography to be pumped into society as "free speech" and promoted in children's classrooms as "sex education?" Are you feeling frustrated and helpless? What can we do to stop this? Take heart! There is something you can do! Let's band together to cut the roots of the problem first! This should be top priority!

The root of the problem is an atheistic, anti-God worldview that is teaching our children from kindergarten through academia that we are nothing but animals. Why be surprised when they act like animals when our society has been teaching them for decades that we are nothing but animals?

WE HAVE THE TRUTH!

In fact, every normal human being has the truth – and knows that we have a Creator. *"For the wrath of God is revealed from heaven against all ungodliness and unrighteousness of men, who suppress the truth in unrighteousness, because what may be known of God is manifest in them, for God has shown it to them. For since the creation of the world His invisible attributes are clearly seen, being understood by the things that are made, even His eternal power and Godhead, so that they are without excuse,*" Romans 1:18-20. The problem is that those who reject the truth and suppress the truth are very good at confusing gullible children (and adults). But God is not the author of confusion! Northwest Science Museum has the Biblical evidence and the scientific evidence to expose the Satanic lies of evolutionism and clarify the TRUTH to children of all ages! **The Bible is true, God is real, Christ is risen, and God Himself is the original scientist!**

NWSM has been exposing Satanic lies and promoting Biblical truth for over five years from our Vision Center at 1831 N. Wildwood in Boise, but it is time for us to expand – greatly expand our exposure, influence, and impact by moving to a larger facility in a better location. We can certainly use your help! Would you like to partner with us to teach the truth by showing the censored science, exposing the lies, and promoting the TRUTH?

Two of my favorite displays at our Vision Center expose the falsehood of the evolutionary timetable of millions of years for the formation of the rock layers in the so-called "geological column":

1. One is a fossil of a fish in the process of swallowing a minnow. This had to happen instantly! The logical and Biblical reason for the rock layers containing billions of fossils is the worldwide flood described in Genesis, Chapters 6-9.

2. We also have the record and evidence of a mammal that ate a baby dinosaur and was buried and fossilized by the Flood. According to the evolutionistic timetable this would be impossible because the evolutionists dogmatically assert that dinosaurs died out many millions of years before mammals "evolved." We have the contrary evidence!

Unalienable Rights!

Remember, the sanctity of life and the sanctity of human sexuality is contingent on the fact that we are created in the image of God, and that He created us male and female! This is God's Truth!

"We hold these truths to be self-evident, that all men are created equal, that they are endowed by their Creator with certain unalienable rights, that among these are Life, Liberty and the Pursuit of Happiness." Declaration of Independence (the most foundational document for our American republic!)

If we continue to allow our unalienable rights to be destroyed by Marxist/atheist indoctrination that discounts our Creator and robs us of our children, then who do we have to blame but ourselves? **Rise up, O men of God! Women of God! Speak up for our Creator! Take a stand for the TRUTH of His Word!**

This is our invitation to you to partner with us to reach the younger generations with the TRUTH and train them to understand and believe the Biblical Christian Worldview instead of the Satanic lies from an atheistic, godless worldview.

Also, I offer you your choice of the following books for an offering of any amount to Overseas Outreach:

Ready to Give an Answer

More than Conquerors in Cultural Clashes

Millions of Miracles: The Evolutionist's Dilemma

Is the Bible without Any Errors?

Note: To accept this offer, please designate which book, provide your mailing address and write to our Overseas Outreach address.

Along with whichever book you choose, I also want to send you Bruce Malone's incredibly inspiring DVD, *Pearls of God,* which shows how creation science verifying the truth of the Word of God is transforming island nations.

Knowledge of the Truth can be Transforming

This true story is from one of my students I met in Ukraine, Paul Sudhakar. He was studying astrophysics in a university and came to my worldview seminar.

"This happened over 25 years ago. There used to be a girl named Padma in a small coastal village in Southern India. She was from a Hindu family. Although from a lower caste, their family was well respected in their village. They were of a good economic and social status. After she finished her high school, she started college in a nearby town. So she had to travel every day from her village to this town to attend classes. It is during this time that she got introduced to Christ. Some of her Christian friends evangelized to her in college and took her to church one Sunday. It was not usual for a Hindu girl to go to church. So, without letting her parents know she went to church one Sunday.

But it wasn't her own interest that drew her to church. It was God's plan. He chose her and called her to Himself. She got drawn by Christ the very first time she went to church. She kept going again and again. And soon she accepted Christ into her life. She had to lie to her parents that she had extra classes in order to go to that town on Sundays to attend church. She accepted Christ into her life and even got baptized, all without the knowledge of her family members. She used to pray quietly after everyone fell asleep. But somehow her family members came to know that she was going to church and that she even got baptized. All of her family members turned against her – her parents, brothers and sisters. Her mom even got paralyzed due to shock upon knowing that she became a Christian!

This was a big blow to her. Her brothers warned that if anything bad happens to their mom, she would be made responsible! At such a hard time, she knelt down and prayed. She asked God "Lord, what should I do now? I want you. Should I lose my mother for You or should I lose You for her and thereby lose everything? Please give me knowledge and strength to bear these tough times." And as she opened her Bible, she saw the verse that says, "If anyone comes to me and does not hate his own father and mother and wife and children and brothers and sisters, yes, and even his own life, he cannot be my disciple." That moment she decided, "no matter what happens, I'm not leaving Christ. Even if it means being hated by my whole family!" But our God is faithful. That very moment, her mom got healed!

But troubles continued to torment this young believer. Her parents started looking for bridegroom for her. She kept rejecting everyone her parents showed her for only one reason – they were not believers! She faced severe accusations from the family for her stubbornness and she faced shame in the society. But she waited on the Lord's promises and believed in His sufficiency. Finally she accepted one guy, which none of her family members liked. He was not rich. His educational qualification was much less than hers (she studied pharmacy!). He didn't have a job. He didn't have a proper house to live in. He didn't have any farm land or cattle (which were (are) the key parameters that decide a person's status in the society, apart from caste). The only qualification he had was that he's Christian!

Having no other choice, her parents reluctantly accepted giving her to him in marriage. They got married in the same church in which she got saved and they started a new life at the guy's place. It wasn't an easy life for them! As I mentioned already, that guy was very poor. They didn't even have a home to live in. A rich guy in their village allowed them to stay in his cattle shed. They cleared a small portion of that shed and lived there! Imagine what a terrible life it was, living with cattle in that dirt and mess with paper and cloth walls! She came from a (although not a very rich family) considerably wealthy family. And here she was, living in a cattle shed! She might have never imagined that something like that would ever happen. All this pain and suffering because she chose Christ!

However, they both remained faithful to God through all their hardships. And our God is a faithful and just God. He won't forsake those who put their hope in Him. He blessed them and brought them up from their poor state. He blessed them with a daughter and a son. And that same son is writing this now! He blessed us to buy a small house in the middle of our village and He gave us a small farm land. And by His grace, we have a pharmacy store too in that same village.

Although we still struggle with finances, we never lacked our daily food or good clothing! His grace has been sufficient all these years and it would be sufficient furthermore too.

He was very gracious to me personally too. He blessed me richly from my childhood. He blessed with some talents and so much of love. It is by His sovereign grace that I, who came from such a small family managed to win third place in an international contest conducted by NASA and by His grace I managed to visit U.S.A. thrice to attend space conferences! He gave me so many things that I never even asked for! But He withheld one thing from me that everyone asks and wishes that He would give to me – health! Yes! From childhood, I suffered from bad health. There was never a year I was completely healthy or without pills. I've been on high power steroid dosages for the past 7 years. I don't know how long more I should continue with them. They did more damage to my body than my illnesses did! They effected my bones, muscles and digestive system. They are the ones responsible for my mood swings too. They made me utterly weak. This recent pain that I was suffering from (still) when you wrote to me first is also a side effect of those drugs. They not only weakened my bones, they also caused problems with my spine. I'm now diagnosed with mild scoliosis and multiple disk damage. That's the reason for the unbearable pain I experienced. I'm taking treatment and I'm doing much better now... I see my parents crying and pleading God for my health. Not just my parents, my friends and many churches as a whole! But God didn't respond yet. Maybe He won't, at all! I'm not even worried about it 'cause I'm strong in my weaknesses. I believe He has a purpose in allowing this sicknesses and troubles in my life. However, I appreciate your prayers. I only have one prayer request. Please pray that my spiritual life won't catch any sickness!"

Note: Paul Sudhakar came to Kharkiv, Ukraine, to study astrophysics, completed his four-year degree, and is now working on his master's degree at a university in Australia. He has a passion for sharing the gospel as well as Christian evidences, so was chosen by his peers to lead the evangelical campus group. Please pray for Paul's ministry, his health, and his future.

Beware of Propaganda Words!

Have you heard of the loud crowd using manipulation and threats with the propaganda words, "homophobia," "islamophobia," etc.? Please, please don't bow to politically loaded, false scare tactics. It is true that a fear can become a phobia, but it is also true that a healthy fear can be good for you – such as a fear of rattlesnakes in the mountains and loose rocks on the edge of cliffs! By the way, do you know where the concept and terminology for "politically correct" comes from? You will find it on page 147 of the little red book entitled, *Quotations from Chairman Mao Tsetung*. Who was Mao Tsetung? No less than the worst mass murderer in history! **"Political correctness" inevitably leads to a suppression of TRUTH!**

As Christians we are commanded to "speak the truth in love," yet sometimes even when we try to speak truth in the most loving manner possible, still we will be falsely accused and labeled as bigots, haters, intolerant do-gooders, etc. (What's wrong with doing good anyway? Isn't that what we are supposed to do?) Jesus "went about doing good", yet the truly intolerant crowd falsely accused Him, mocked Him, spat on Him, beat Him, and subjected Him to the most shameful and cruel death possible. Jesus told us that the servant is not above his Master. So what are we to do? Wipe the spit off, ignore the mocking, and keep speaking the truth in love! And we may need to practice praying, "Father forgive them – for they know not what they do!" when we hear of or read about other Christians being falsely accused and abused by the intolerant "tolerant" troop. Let's also remember what Paul wrote to Timothy: *"I solemnly urge you in the presence of God and Christ Jesus, who will someday judge the living and the dead when he comes to set up his Kingdom: Preach the Word of God. Be prepared, whether the time is favorable or not. Patiently correct, rebuke, and encourage your people with good teaching. For a time is coming when people will no longer listen to sound and wholesome teaching. They will follow their own desires and will look for teachers who will tell them whatever their itching ears want to hear. They will reject the truth and chase after myths. But you should keep a clear mind in every situation. Don't be afraid of suffering for the Lord. Work at telling others the Good News, and fully carry out the ministry God has given you."* 2 Timothy 4:1-5 (NLT)

The Truth about Tough Love

Most adults and even many children recognize that sometimes "love must be tough!" Parents, police, pastors, coaches, teachers, animal trainers – and all rational individuals know that to discipline someone and to train anyone to become good, better or best in his or her obedience and skills requires tough love. However, in our socially warped, so-called "politically correct" world, tough love is not only being neglected – it is being bad-mouthed and falsified as hate speech. For example, it's likely that I may be maligned and charged with hate speech because I refuse to bow to the propaganda term "gay" as proper terminology for a practice that God in His Word calls "sodomy" and "abomination." I believe God means what He says: "If any man speak, let him speak as the oracles of God." 1 Peter 4:11 The NIV renders this passage: "If anyone speak, he should do it as one speaking the very words of God"! The original and actual meaning of the word "gay" is "carefree and happy." Some of our relatives have wandered down the immoral path of homosexuality. Carefree and happy? Hardly!

Tough Love Applied

The Word of God also teaches: *"Do you not know that the unrighteous will not inherit the kingdom of God? Do not be deceived. Neither fornicators, nor idolaters, nor adulterers, nor homosexuals, nor sodomites, nor thieves, nor covetous, nor drunkards, nor revilers, nor extortioners will inherit the kingdom of God. And such were some of you. But you were washed, but you were sanctified, but you were justified in the name of the Lord Jesus and by the Spirit of our God.*" 1 Corinthians 6:9-11. Is it "hate speech" for devoted Christians to love a drunkard enough to invite him to turn from his sin, to come Home to Jesus, to repent, to be baptized, and to enroll in rehab and recovery classes to change his corrupted habits? No! Absolutely not! This is the application of tough love! Shouldn't Christians also have the same compassion for those trapped in any form of sexual immorality? Especially if God labels it an abomination? The bottom line is that "all have sinned and fallen short of the glory of God." All of us are sinners, but some of us sinners have been saved by the grace of God – and our task is to invite others to come Home to Jesus to be forgiven, freed from the chains of sin and death so we can experience "the peace that passes all understanding"! Doesn't that better fit the definition of "carefree and happy"? Even when we face tough situations, including false accusations and persecution, Jesus said: *"Blessed are those who are persecuted for righteousness' sake, for theirs is the kingdom of heaven. Blessed are you when they revile and persecute you, and say all kinds of evil against you falsely for My sake. Rejoice and be exceedingly glad, for great is your reward in heaven, for so they persecuted the prophets who were before you."* Matthew 5:10-12. (Some translations say "happy" instead of "blessed.") Do want to be "carefree and happy"? Turn from your sin (repent), be baptized into Christ, receive the forgiveness of your sin and the gift of the Holy Spirit (Acts 2:38), then cast all your cares on Jesus because He cares for you! Trust Him with your life, your finances, your relationships, your past, your present, your future – your everything! That is the way to be "carefree and happy" here and now – with a glorious future of hope, peace and joy to anticipate! Wow! What are you waiting for? These are the benefits of tough love! **When Jesus hung on the cross in agony of body and soul – that was tough love paying the penalty of your sin - and mine! That's grace! Now out of a heart bursting with gratitude, let's rise up and serve Him with passion and purity until the day He bursts through the clouds on the white horse conquering and to conquer!**

Forgiven! Cleansed! Redeemed!

(Poem by Shasta Hutton – Based on her Grandpa's Own Thoughts)

Sometimes I think about the things,
I've done wrong in my life,
About the times I've done the things,
That cause much pain and strife.

I feel so bad and hate those things.
I'd change them if I could,
Erase them all and start again,
And do the things I should.

I go to God and cry to Him,
"I cannot change the past.
I can't undo the hurt I've caused.
Those things will always last."

He draws me close and says to me,
"I know, my child. I know,
But that is why I shed My blood,
And still I love you so.

And all those evil things you've done,
And all you've yet to do,
Were washed, forgiven, and made clean.
You can begin anew.

And though the past can't be undone,
Redeemed it still can be.
So do not fret. Do not despair.
The future's yet to see.

Together we'll go forward now,
Into a hurting land,
And work the fields of hurting souls,
And take them by the hand.

We'll show them how they too can be,
Forgiven and made new.
And since you've shared their darksome path,
They'll listen now to you."

And as my Father speaks these words,
My faith's again made strong.
I've been forgiven, cleansed, redeemed.
With Him I can go on.

Though consequences still remain,
I'll put the past behind,
And serve my Father, God, and King,
With heart and soul and mind.

Napoleon's Perspective About Jesus and the Bible After His Waterloo

Napoléon is recorded to have said: "I know men, and I tell you Jesus Christ was not a man. (Not 'a mere man!' R.D.)

Superficial minds see a resemblance between Christ and the founders of empires and the gods of other religions. That resemblance does not exist.

There is between Christianity and other religions the distance of infinity.

Alexander, Caesar, Charlemagne and I founded empires. But on what did we rest the creations of our genius? Upon sheer force. Jesus Christ alone founded His empire upon love; and at this hour millions of men will die for Him...

From the first day to the last He is the same; majestic and simple; infinitely firm and infinitely gentle. He proposes to our faith a series of mysteries and commands with authority that we should believe them, giving no other reason than those tremendous words, 'I am God.'

The Bible contains a complete series of acts and of historical men to explain time and eternity, such as no other religion has to offer... for everything in it is grand and worthy of God.

The more I consider the Gospel, the more I am assured that there is nothing there which is not beyond the march of events and above the human mind. Even the impious themselves have never dared to deny the sublimity of the Gospel, which inspires them with a sort of compulsory veneration. What happiness that Book procures for those who believe it!"

Remember Me, America

Remember me, America.
I was once your son.
I fought and died in Valley Forge
With General Washington.

I was there again in Gettysburg
On that tragic, tragic day,
When brother fought against brother.
The blue against the gray.

I was there with Teddy Roosevelt,
A charge called San Juan Hill.
Some came back to fight again,
But I just lay there still.

I was there at Pearl Harbor,
On a day called Infamy.
And I'm still there with my shipmates,
At the bottom of the sea.

D-day, June 6, 1944.
We stormed the beaches of Normandy.
We fought uphill every inch of the way.
We routed those Germans and we pushed them back,
But oh, the price we had to pay.

I heard the Seals say one night in Korea,
"We can take it. I know we will."

So I died again in a place they named Porkchop Hill.

Vietnam, Vietnam, when will we ever learn?
I'm one of many thousands who did not return.
I left my town, my wife, my kids, my home so dear for war.

And died again in a scud attack in a place called Desert Storm.
So in my eternity, my thoughts will go to thee.
I won't forget you, America.
But please, America, do not forget me.

"Freedom is not free!" This quotation is to remind us that although it may be free to us now – others paid the price (sometimes a terrible price). So, not only on Memorial Day, Flag Day, and the 4th of July should we celebrate our freedom and remember those who risked and sacrificed life and limbs for our freedom – but every day. Especially let's remember that our freedom in Christ from the bondage of sin, death and hell was paid for by the precious blood of Jesus! Can you hear Jesus say, "Remember Me, Christian"?

"Stand fast therefore in the liberty by which Christ has made us free, and do not be entangled again with a yoke of bondage." Galatians 5:1

"And if you call on the Father, who without partiality judges according to each one's work, conduct yourselves throughout the time of your stay here in fear; knowing that you were not redeemed with corruptible things, like silver or gold, from your aimless conduct received by tradition from your fathers, but with the precious blood of Christ, as of a lamb without blemish and without spot." 1 Peter 1:17-19

> **"Compared with the ancient civilizations, America was born yesterday. But, and here is the rub – she is dying today, and she will be dead tomorrow unless there is a spiritual awakening."**
>
> ~ *Leonard Ravenhill (one of England's foremost evangelists),*
> *America Is Too Young to Die, 1979, p. 29*

Rick Hughes points out that when God created humans, He gave us two ends: one end we use to sit on and the other we use to think with. Our joy and success in life choices depend on acting wisely about which end we use. Are we content to sit on one end of our anatomy numbing the other end with foolish sitcoms and/or violent video games, etc.? He also quoted someone who mentioned that arrogance plus ignorance equal AI – Artificial Intelligence. Why not activate genuine intelligence by listening to God's Word and obeying Him?

My Tribute

I am glad to begin my tribute with the words from Andre Crouch's famous song, "My Tribute", "If I never had a problem, I wouldn't know that He could solve them.....To God be the glory for the things He has done!" Amen!

When I was a senior in high school in Longmont, Colorado, back in 1961, I had a problem. It was springtime, I was to graduate soon, and I didn't know what I was going to do after graduation. But God had a plan! He sent Kenneth Beckman to Longmont for an evangelistic meeting, which changed the course of my life.

One Friday evening that previous winter, I had walked out of the Teen Canteen to quietly reflect on Talmage Pace's words to our youth group, "Don't ever put yourself in a situation where you would be ashamed to be found when Jesus returns!" That cold clear evening I could see the Teen Canteen half a block away on one side and our church building one block away on the other side - and I knew that I had to make a decision. I could not keep calling myself a Christian, yet keep living on the fence. That evening I decided that Jesus Christ means more to me than all my worldly pleasures, friends, and compromises.

Then one evening as I walked out of the evangelistic meeting, Talmage Pace asked me where I was going to go to Bible college. I told him, "I don't know" - but the idea lodged in my mind and heart. I was impressed by Kenneth Beckman's fervency and scholarship - and my oldest sister lived in Boise, so I chose to come to Boise Bible College.

For this I am forever grateful!

My classes and experiences at Boise Bible College and the church at 18th and Eastman in Boise (which sponsored BBC) gave me a solid foundation of Biblical worldview and missionary fervency that has stabilized my life and motivated me to love, worship and serve my awesome Lord Jesus Christ for the rest of my life. Not only all of that, God had Della Qualey waiting for me when I arrived. A year and a half later she became Della Deighton (December 14, 1962) and she has been a beautiful part of my life as my wife, life partner, and co-worker for over 53 years now. So, my gratitude is deep and genuine. Thank you, Boise Bible College! (The nickname "Boise Bridal College" was not given in vain!)

Something else foundational to my life transpired in the evangelistic meeting with Kenneth Beckman during my senior year of high school. One evening my friend, Ron Smith stepped out into the aisle, followed by his wife, Judy, to come to the front of the church to receive Jesus as Lord. Only a few months before, I had made my first stumbling effort to witness to Ron while we were duck hunting. When I saw Ron walk out and Judy running behind him, I felt like my heart was going to jump out of my body. **It was an even greater thrill than coming to Jesus myself! Friends, if you are searching for a greater purpose and thrill than walking with the King of the universe and sharing Jesus with others, you are on a dead-end path!**

I was one of those kids who came to Boise Bible College for a year to get a better Biblical foundation for my life, but within two months **I knew that growing in the knowledge of God and sharing Jesus is my life.** In the youth meetings at church and at BBC events we often sang, "You never mentioned Him to me...you met me day by day, you knew I was astray, but you never mentioned Him to me." What a convicting, motivating song! I did not realized how convicting and motivating until I returned to Longmont after my first year at BBC and learned that Earl Kolb and Johnny Walker were both killed in the same motorcycle accident a short time before. These were two guys I went to school with...that I graduated with - but I never mentioned Him to either of them. **I vowed to never let that happen again!**

When I returned to BBC for my second year, there were four of us from Longmont enrolling as students - and later there were five. Why? **Because there are some things too good to keep to ourselves.**

I want to conclude with a tribute to my friends, Dick and Maudine Ady, founders of World English Institute, which God is using to reach multitudes in 190 countries around the earth through combined English and Bible correspondence courses. In the editorial for their first quarter update of 2016, Dick wrote:

> "....In 1985, the Times-Reporter of New Philadelphia, Ohio, reported that a group of 400 people gathered around a municipal swimming pool in New Orleans to celebrate the first summer in memory that no one had drowned in city pools. The crowd that gathered included 200 life guards. As the party broke up and the four life guards on duty cleared the pool, they found the fully-clothed body of thirty-one year old Jerome Moody in the deep end of the pool. He had drowned surrounded by life guards celebrating their successful season.
>
> **"Let us not make the same mistake by ignoring people who are downing in sin and letting them perish while we enjoy life and celebrate our successes."**

Can you imagine the impact it would make on our families, co-workers, churches, and neighborhoods if each of us adopted Paul's purpose for living? It is clearly given in Colossians 1:27-29:

> "To them God willed to make known what are the riches of the glory of this mystery among the Gentiles: which is **Christ in you, the hope of glory. Him we preach, warning every man and teaching every man in all wisdom that we may present every man perfect in Christ Jesus.** To this end I also labor, striving according to His working which works in me mightily."

Tribute to the Bible

"This Book Contains:

The mind of God, the state of man, the way of salvation, doom of sinners, and happiness of believers. Its doctrines are holy, its precepts are binding, its histories are true, and its decisions are immutable. Read it to be wise, believe it to be safe, and practice it to be holy. It contains light to direct you, food to support you and comfort to cheer you. It is the traveler's map, the pilgrim's staff, the pilot's compass, the soldier's sword and the Christian's charter. Here Paradise is restored, Heaven opened, and the gates of hell disclosed. Christ is its Grand Subject, our good its design, and the glory of God its end. It should fill the memory, rule the heart, and guide the feet. Read it slowly, frequently, prayerfully. It is a mine of wealth, a paradise of glory, and a river of pleasure. It is given you in life, will be open at the Judgment and be remembered forever. It involves the highest responsibility, rewards the greatest labor, and condemns all who trifle with its holy contents."

"I'm Glad I'm Alive"

When our granddaughter, Trinity Hope, was seven years old, she came bounding through our house announcing, "I'm glad I'm alive!" On this earth cursed because of sin, which is so plagued with sickness, sorrow, grief, discouragement, despondency, depression, despair and suicide – isn't it refreshing to hear (or read) "I'm glad I'm alive!"?

Trinity's middle name is "Hope," and her first name is a reflection of the fact that Almighty God is Himself unity in diversity as Father, Son, and Holy Spirit. Unity in His diversity produces hope, joy, peace – the components of abundant life. Yes, He is the author and producer of life – physically, spiritually, abundantly and eternally.

Trinity understands that even when we (her parents, grandparents, teachers, etc.) must discipline her – it is because we love her. She knows we love her, and God loves her – deeply and truly. Do you know that? Have you submitted your will to His will? Do you feel like bounding through your home announcing, "I'm glad I'm alive!"? Ponder this: *"Whoever believes in the Son of God has the testimony in himself. Whoever does not believe God has made him a liar, because he has not believed in the testimony that God has borne concerning His Son. And this is the testimony, that God gave us eternal life, and this life is in His Son. Whoever has the Son has life; whoever does not have the Son of God does not have life. I write these things to you who believe in the name of the Son of God, that you may know that you have eternal life."* 1 John 5:10-13 (ESV).

Are you accepting and rejoicing in the fact that our Father's discipline in your life is because He loves you? This will be your practical application of your knowledge of the truth.

Questions for Chapter 5

1. What did the apostle Paul tell Timothy is "good and acceptable in the sight of God our Savior"?

2. Can you relate to the frustration of "being tired of the devolving of our formerly great American culture"? If so, what should be our top priority?

3. How can we know that we have the truth? (Hint – check Romans 1:18-20 and the information we have at NWSM. I gave you two examples.)

4. According to our American Declaration of Independence, where do our unalienable rights come from?

5. What impacted you most in the testimony Paul Sudhakar shared about his family?

6. Where does the concept and terminology for "politically correct" come from, and why is it dangerous?

7. When we "speak the truth in love," should we expect that people will always receive it in love and appreciate our loving concern?

8. How should we respond when we are misunderstood, mistreated and falsely accused?

9. What is the truth about tough love and who has best demonstrated that tough love?

10. What do you think was the source of Trinity's joy expressed by, "I'm glad I'm alive!"? Do you have this joy in your soul?

Bonus Questions

1. Concerning the quotations from Napoleon, what was the most impressive to you?

2. What is the message to our hearts from the poem, "Remember Me, America"?

CHAPTER 6

Clinching Our Convictions

To give you even more evidence of the cultural clashes and social insanity bogging down our formerly great country in the swamp of critical corruption, I want to begin this chapter with an amazingly insightful article by Larry Spargimino, published in the August 2019 issue of *Prophetic Observer*.

"Male and Female Created He Them"

"There are statements in the Bible that we often gloss over and even wonder why they are there. It seems to say something that is so obvious, who would question such an obvious truth? The above quotation from Genesis 1:27 is one of those statements. Isn't there a universal unanimity that God made men and women, and that's the way it is?

However, one of the things that I have learned in a new and fresh way is that 'ALL Scripture is given by inspiration of God, and is PROFITABLE' (2 Timothy 3:16). Believe it or not there are some people – and their number is growing worldwide – who think that 'male and female' is just a suggestion. They believe it's not biology that matters, but one's perception – 'Anatomically I'm a boy but I won't be happy until my anatomy matches my feelings. I need to transition!'

Senseless Mutilation or Needful Therapy?

If you were a surgeon and someone asked you to cut off a perfectly healthy arm or leg because that individual feels that it is terribly 'wrong' for that arm or leg to be there, and his psychiatrist said that individual would be better adjusted if that offending limb were removed, would you perform the requested surgery? The individual's psychiatrist even warned that if you did not remove that body part that individual might be forced to commit suicide.

There is a mental condition known as Body Integrity Identity Disorder (BIID). People who struggle with it feel they are not supposed to have a certain part of their body. 'As a general rule,' writes John Haskins for Townhall.com, 'doctors won't remove a healthy body part; so these poor deluded people crush, mangle, burn, or otherwise deliberately destroy their own arms or legs in order to get a surgeon to slice them off.'

To make the question a little more relevant to what follows in this piece – Supposing you are a surgeon and the person who is going to have the body part removed is a minor child. You have been told by the mother who wants you to cut off this perfectly healthy body part, that this child has told her some things that would lead her to conclude that the presence of this body part is causing emotional distress. She is a pediatrician and certainly 'knows best.' Would you remove this healthy body part?

Stranger Than Fiction – But Tragically Real

Jeff Younger has two sons, James and Jude. Jeff is particularly concerned about James. Jeff's ex-wife, Anne Georgulas, MD, a pediatrician in Dallas, Texas, affiliated with Dallas Children's Hospital, began dressing James as a girl when he was three. She began to call James by the name Luna and began taking him to therapy with a gender-transition therapist and enrolled him in school as a 'girl.' In school James/

Luna uses the girls' bathroom and is known by teachers and staff as one of the 'girls.'

Georgulas, James's mother, is seeking to terminate the parental rights of James' father, Jeff Younger, because the child behaves as a boy – his biological sex – when he is with his father. Younger almost ended up in jail because he took James to the barbershop where he got his son a boys' haircut. Georgulas also wants Younger to pay for their son's counseling with a therapist who will affirm his transgender identity, and for transgender hormonal treatments which may begin at age eight. Breitbart states that Younger is shocked and stated, 'Few things are more important to people than the care and rearing of their young. The courts are entertaining government suppression of some of the most fundamental practices and traditions of American families.' In a phone interview, Younger told this author that there are 250 children in Texas who are currently awaiting to be 'transitioned.'

The court has prohibited James' father from dressing him as a boy or from sharing Bible-based and biologically-based scientific teachings on sexuality, even though family friends who have observed James when he is in his father's care affirm that he dresses and behaves as a boy by his own choosing.

James is currently being socially transitioned by Georgulas – wearing a dress, being called by a female name – but in two years he will begin a regimen of chemical transitioning and 'chemical castration.' Medical research suggests that hormone blockers can cause serious damage including permanent sterility and bone density issues, just to name a few. However, since science doesn't seem to matter to these people, science is 'irrelevant' and will not be used to halt a destructive ideology.

The savejames.com website cites a *Journal of Medicine* study that shows: 'Puberty blocker chemical castration is an ineffective treatment for gender dysphoria. None of the children who were chemically castrated got better. In fact, they got worse and moved on to surgical transition.' In other words, they were castrated. People who are pushing transgenderism don't like to use the word 'castration.' They know it's a red flag. However, in my research for this piece, transitioning leaves the individual dissatisfied and troubled with his/her biological gender. The only thing that will produce a measure of relief is castration, or breast removal in the case of teen girls.

For readers who want to learn more about where the transgender craze is taking us, and how it is tragically impacting lives in Texas at the present time, please refer to savejames.com. This website is extensive, and contains medical reports, resources, and testimony, and also a 'donate' button for those who wish to help Jeffrey Younger with the immense legal fees he is facing in his attempt to save his son.

There are several links to additional resources which provide medical testimony that not a single long-term study supports risky medical interventions that are being contemplated for James. Girls may have their breasts removed at age 13 and their uterus at 16. Teen boys are having their male parts removed after their sixteenth birthday.

Disappointed By Transitioning

Walt Heyer, who transitioned and formally identified as a woman but has de-transitioned and now provides support to people who regret their sex change, knows firsthand what it feels like to want to be a woman. It's not just his own story he knows but has received correspondence from hundreds of men and women who realized their transition wasn't delivering all that it promised, and actually caused additional problems.

In his book, *Trans Life Survivors,* Heyer writes that 'a questionable diagnosis locks a vulnerable child into an alternate gender identity long before they can understand what is happening or where it might lead. It's up to the adults to observe the child carefully, consider and question the grey areas, and ultimately guard innocent children against hasty diagnoses and conclusions about something as fundamental as their gender identity.'

Satan's Devastating War On The Mind

The human mind is a beautiful creation of God, but easily swayed. The power of suggestion has been demonstrated many times over. The eating disorders with which teen girls struggle occur in clusters of girls and their friends, showing gender confusion often comes not from within, but from without. Predictably, gender confusion is an outgrowth of gay activism. Once they attempted to redefine marriage, they also rendered gender meaningless within marriage, since for them marriage was no longer the union of a man and a woman but the union of any two people. Sadly, once gender is meaningless within marriage, you render gender meaningless within society.

Have you ever been surprised at how many strange ideas are now being offered as the solution to all of our problems, nonsensical ideas causing a multitude of unwanted consequences, ideas that are now being sanctioned by the so-called intellectual elite? We can name a few such as open borders, voting rights for non-citizens, sanctuary cities and states that invite criminals - and now a court that is forcing a father to pay for his son's transitioning – the new meme seems to be, 'Hate thy body. Biology doesn't matter.'

Young people who are no longer taught that the fear of the Lord is the beginning of wisdom (Proverbs 9:10) have a bizarre idea, and that idea is nurtured and fed and encouraged to come out of the misty shadows of fantasy to become their new reality. Indeed, 'the god of this world hath blinded the minds of them which believe not' (2 Corinthians 4:4).

This culture shift into madness gives a deeper insight in what it means to be saved. Salvation is not only deliverance from hell – though we must never diminish the significance of that! – but salvation also means getting plugged in to reality.

Reality is knowing, first, that you are a sinner hopelessly lost for time and eternity; second, you need God's help NOW! Third, you are not 'god' and don't decide what is right and wrong; fourth, if left on your own and not enlightened by the Holy Spirit you will give a totally confused and miserable existence; fifth, God is long-suffering and unbelievably patient and gracious, but a day is coming when His wrath will be revealed and nothing will stop it. You are plugged into reality when you cry out, 'Lord, what must I do to be saved?' and receive the gift of salvation that is freely offered to all (Ephesians 2:8-9).

Please check out the website savejames.com. Pray for James and his father Jeff Younger, and for all the others, and for the millions of boys and girls who are in great danger. The battle that is not fought is always lost.

History is replete with medical insanities. Frontal lobotomies to treat mental illness. Forced sterilization to control 'undesirable' people groups. The infamous Tuskegee Experiment. Cruel, indefensible, unscientific, unethical medical procedures were performed for years. The screams of the victims still echo in the corridors of time. Why did it take so long for the termination of these barbaric procedures?" ("Male and Female Created He Them," by Pastor Larry Spargimino, Ph.D., August 2019 *Prophetic Observer.* Used by permission.)

Caution and Compassion

What Larry has clearly and concisely exposed to us in this outstanding article is the fact that we are faced with a very real and present danger in the cultural clashes over LGBTQ ideology and agenda. I realize that I need – and perhaps all of us who are conservative Americans and Christians committed to the Biblical Christian Worldview need - is to remember Paul's words of caution and instruction to Timothy along with his exhortation to preach the Word, contend for the faith, and oppose false doctrines. Therefore, as we contend for the truth and seek to speak the truth clearly, boldly and lovingly, let's not forget this:

"But avoid foolish and ignorant disputes, knowing that they generate strife. And a servant of the Lord must not quarrel but be gentle to all, able to teach, patient, in humility correcting those who are in opposition, if God perhaps will grant them repentance, so that they may know the truth, and that they may come to their senses and escape the snare of

the devil, having been taken captive by him to do his will." 2 Timothy 2:23-26

Clarity in the Midst of Caution and Compassion

The September-October 2019 issue of *Answers* magazine is entitled "Culture in Crisis" with the sub-heading "The Creation Based Perspective on Gender and Sexuality." I can highly recommend for you to get your own copy because the articles are excellent. Especially clarifying is the article "The Biology of Gender" by Dr. Georgia Purdom. She wrote: "**Biology and God's Word are clear – there are only two genders/sexes.**" Isn't this the obvious, factual truth that most of us already knew? But isn't it so refreshing to read these clarifying words from a medical doctor who has the courage and conviction to speak truth and be willing to face the outrage of those pushing the LGBTQ agenda? Near the end of her article is a very helpful and clarifying section about the abnormalities from mutations, etc. (since we live on a cursed earth). She titled that section "What About Gender/Sex Abnormalities?"

Very Good!

It was after God's creation of human beings as male and female that He pronounced His creation **very good**! Since God is not the author of confusion, how does He regard those who do introduce confusion about His very good creation? That is a very important question for those introducing gender as something subjective and distinct from biological sexual distinctions.

Let's Pray for Discernment!

Are you aware that the meaning of certain words has been distorted and that these have become propaganda words used for manipulation by those promoting the so-called "liberal" agenda? (Liberal is one of those words – its actual meaning is "generous.") "Gay," "tolerant," and "discriminate" are three more of these words. Is discrimination always bad? Definition #2 of the word discriminate in my dictionary is "the ability to make or perceive distinctions; perception; discernment." We cannot possibly live wise and godly lives without discernment; that is, without the ability to draw a distinction (discriminate) between truth and falsehood, wisdom and folly, good and evil, or better and best. Yes, let's pray for discernment. In my research for this chapter and my desire to apply caution and compassion to the touchy subject of gender dysphoria, I decided to read a book that was recommended in a book on apologetics and outreach to millennials. This next section is my attempt to also apply discernment to what I've read while searching for caution and compassion.

Understanding Gender Dysphoria?

Mark Yarhouse is a psychology professor at Wheaton College. In his 2015 book, *Understanding Gender Dysphoria,* he lists three frameworks for viewing and understanding "gender identity concerns": 1. **The integrity framework**, which focuses on the fact that God Himself created mankind male and female and declared His work "very good." This viewpoint highlights the sanctity of sex, marriage and family as God's creation by His wise design. 2. **The disability framework**, which acknowledges and recognizes that we live on a cursed earth that is fallen and subject to death, decay and harmful mutations. This is also part of a Biblical Christian Worldview – that we no longer live in a perfect paradise as our Creator originally designed. Therefore, because of harmful mutations and genetic or chromosome imbalances, there are sometimes babies born with mixed sexual identity. Mark Yarhouse wrote: "An intersex condition is one in which at birth an infant was unable to be identified as male or female because of ambiguous genitalia." (*Understanding Gender Dysphoria,* p. 90) In such cases, both parents and doctors need extreme wisdom, caution and compassion. (Our first granddaughter, Rachel, was born with Trisomy 18, a chromosome disorder with severe consequences, but not concerning her gender.) 3. **The diversity framework** – which I consider to be highly suspicious and much more subjective rather than objective like the other two frameworks. I believe that this "diversity framework" is where heavy doses of humanistic psychology, feelings over facts, and propaganda words come into play.

When I read a book, I tend to get into discussions with the author, and I give no apology for that. In fact, I believe it is both exhorted and commanded in Scripture. 1 Thessalonians 5:21 says, *"Test all things; hold fast what is good."* Luke commended the Jews of the synagogue in Berea by writing: *"These were more fair-minded than those in Thessalonica, in that they received the word with all readiness, and searched the Scriptures daily to find out whether these things were so."* Acts 17:11 Let's take this as an exhortation to do likewise.

One reviewer for this book wrote: "Mark Yarhouse has written yet another important contribution to the church's discussion about LGBTQ issues, this time focusing specifically on questions related to transgender people. This book is informed by studious attention to the Bible, sound theological reasoning and deep psychological wisdom, all of which is sifted through a compassionate heart that wants to see people experience the deep love of Christ..."

I also had a discussion with this reviewer. The problem is that most "psychological wisdom" is strongly tainted with the wisdom of this world through the main leaders of "psychology." The true psychology is found in the Word of God, for the word "psychology" means "the study of the soul." Who knows more about the soul than the Genius who created us?

Now, far more important than what I wrote, here is what the Spirit of God inspired Paul to write: *"Beware lest anyone cheat you through philosophy and empty deceit, according to the tradition of men, according to the basic principles of the world, and not according to Christ. For in Him dwells all the fullness of the Godhead bodily; and you are complete in Him, who is the head of all principality and power."* Colossians 2:8-10

I wrote to Mark Yarhouse and commended him for his compassionate manner, but also expressed my concern about some of his opinions. He replied in a very humble and kind letter – without being defensive. I appreciate deeply his heart and his manner, yet I'm just as deeply concerned with the direction he is attempting to take his readers. I wrote to him again to express this concern and to invite him to read and critique what I'm writing, especially if I've written anything that is not accurate Biblically. I've also pointed out to him that although compassion may be his strong point in connecting with people, it may be his weak spot in earnestly contending for the faith. Why? I can relate because Della sometimes points out to me that my compassion for hurting people can easily make me a sucker for a sob story. I've had to learn and re-learn that love must be tough when reaching out to prisoners. (Some of them are excellent con-artists.) Children also can be expert manipulators with their sob stories.

Here are my most serious concerns about the book, *Understanding Gender Dysphoria:*

1. Mark Yarhouse promotes the idea that there is a distinction between gender and sex, but he gives no Biblical verification for this assertion.

2. Mark leans heavily on the diversity framework for much of what he says in the book, but he gave me no Biblical reason to believe it is true. Therefore, in view of the Holy Spirit's warning in Colossians 2:8-10, I reject it as humanistic philosophy rather than Biblical truth.

3. Although the book is entitled, *Understanding Gender Dysphoria,* the more I read, the more misunderstanding and confusion I found.

4. One of my heroes of the faith, W. Carl Ketcherside, wrote that the difference between Jesus and the philosophers was that the philosophers could take a simple subject and in attempting to sound profound could confuse everyone, but Jesus could take profound

truth and make it clear even to a child. I found more confusion than clarity in Mark's book. Whose pattern is he following?

5. My most serious concern of all is that by adopting "The Diversity Framework" as a third frame of reference, he is adding another authority apart from and outside of the Bible. Why should we reject the Roman Catholic Church as an outside authority along with the Bible and yet accept the Diversity Framework as valid? Shall we ask those who are in court battles with the LGBTQ agenda for their perspective on this?

Actually, factually, since there is no biological basis nor Biblical basis for the "Diversity Framework," then isn't it logical to conclude that it is pure fantasy based on subjective feelings, sob stories, and humanistic psychology (philosophy)?

I have a strong suspicion that at the base of most sob stories we are likely to find a root of bitterness, a root of self-pity, and a root of manipulation. Let's reject the manipulation and cut the roots!

When I was 12 years, old my dad had his left arm ripped off his body and all the flesh peeled off his left ankle and foot in a tractor accident. As a veteran, he could have lived off government funds for the rest of his life, but he refused to do so. In fact, he went back to work six months after his accident and continued to earn his own income until retirement well past his 65th birthday. I saw true grit at home long before seeing John Wayne's movie, *True Grit*. Maybe, with this background, you may understand why I'm not moved to tears by a guy with a sob story, "I'm a woman trapped in a man's body!" (Sniff, sniff. Poor me!) The verse I think of for that guy would be 1 Corinthians 16:13: "Be watchful, stand firm in the faith, act like men, be strong." (ESV) The question I would like to ask him is – could you picture our Lord Jesus beaten, bruised, mocked, spit upon, and hanging on the cross to pay for our sins and give Him that sob story?

From my own ministry experience, I can testify that many of those who came for counseling were not looking for sound Biblical advice. Rather they were looking for a handout, or for someone in a position of authority to validate their sob stories and agree with their excuses.

I do want to obey God's Word to "bear one another's burdens, and so fulfill the law of Christ" (Galatians 6:2), but I also want to obey Him about being wise and discerning about the use of time, talent, and treasure. This is a stewardship issue, and I want to be a good steward of everything our Father has committed to His trust. Too often I have already allowed con artists with sob stories to drain from me time, attention, and money that could have been more wisely invested for the good of Christ's Kingdom.

While we were living in Gresham, Oregon, a frail, shy young man from India cautiously visited our congregation a couple times. When I followed up to try to reach him and teach him the gospel, I found out that he was actually the sex slave of a middle-aged man who had abandoned and divorced his own wife in order to indulge himself in the homosexual lifestyle. Ironically, when I confronted this guy and tried to lead him to repent, he pulled a sob story on me. I didn't fall for that sob story, and the guy didn't repent. Neither did the shy, frail young man from India.

It was also during our years in Gresham that I personally saw and experienced the hatred of the intolerant "tolerant" troop who like to call Christians a "hate group."

I will venture to offer you a few more thoughts to ponder about the subject of gender dysphoria:

1. Do you think it is wise to separate the word "gender" from the word "sex?"? Isn't that simply word manipulation by humanistic psychology techniques? The clearest definition in my dictionary

for the word "gender" is the word "sex." Is it logical to teach vulnerable kids (or adults) that you can be a different gender than your biological sex? (But then, what does logic, scientific fact, and Biblical truth have to do with the craziness of believing whatever you choose to believe? Aren't feelings more important than facts in our sensitive society?)

2. Do you also wonder how many cases of gender dysphoria would be cured if an individual would deeply and truly repent for the sin of being an ungrateful complainer and started praising and thanking our Father in Heaven for who He created him (or her) to be? All the Israelites over 20 years old (except Joshua and Caleb) died in the wilderness for their unbelief and griping. **Wouldn't we all be far better off if we just obey God's Word?** *"Rejoice always, pray without ceasing, in everything give thanks; for this is the will of God in Christ Jesus for you."* 1 Thessalonians 5:16-18

3. With a little more reflection, I realize that since there are multiple causes for gender dysphoria and our Father is the only one with complete understanding, our first response should be earnest prayer for those entrapped in this distress – coupled with caution and compassion.

Three Pertinent Scriptures About Scripture

"For the word of God is living and powerful, and sharper than any two-edged sword, piercing even to the division of soul and spirit, and of joints and marrow, and is a discerner of the thoughts and intents of the heart. And there is no creature hidden from His sight, but all things are naked and open to the eyes of Him to whom we must give account." Heb. 4:11-13

"For this reason we also thank God without ceasing, because when you received the word of God which you heard from us, you welcomed it not as the word of men, but as it is in truth, the word of God, which also effectively works in you who believe." 1 Thessalonians 2:13

"and that from childhood you have known the Holy Scriptures, which are able to make you wise for salvation through faith which is in Christ Jesus. All Scripture is given by inspiration of God, and is profitable for doctrine, for reproof, for correction, for instruction in righteousness, that the man of God may be complete, thoroughly equipped for every good work." 2 Timothy 3:15-17

Potent Questions About the Sufficiency of Scripture

1. Since the Word of God (Bible) is sufficient to make me complete as a man of God – why do I need another source of authority for my life and my ministry? (Whether the *Book of Mormon, Watchtower,* or human psychology books?)

2. Since the Word of God is sufficient to make me thoroughly equipped for every good work, would that not include counseling confused individuals – even if they are confused about gender issues?

3. Since the Word of God makes it clear that Luke was a physician as well as a traveling missionary with the Apostle Paul, wouldn't I be wise to get a doctor's help for someone dealing with hormonal, nutritional issues (especially a doctor who studies nutrition)?

Next, you will find 15 of my core convictions which shape my life, my ministry and my priorities. I hope that this will help you clarify and clinch your own core convictions, and help you learn to discern the difference between convictions and opinions. Opinions should remain flexible and changeable based on new information, but convictions should be based on the solid Rock of our Lord Jesus Christ and His immutable Word of Truth. Opinions are not worth dying for, but convictions are! Convictions are what transform wimps into winners! Convictions are what transform weak-willed, wishy-washy, half-hearted Christians into blazing, bold beacons of Truth. Convictions forged by the fire of the Holy Spirit and the truth of Jesus' resurrection transformed Peter from being self-confident to being Christ-confident and from being a blatant betrayer to be a brazenly bold believer! By His Spirit and His Truth, He can change you from a weak-willed wonder to a powerful possessor and confessor of His truth! Do you feel like a failure rather than a witness for Jesus? The Spirit of God transformed Peter from a self-filled flop to a Spirit-filled flame – and He wants to do the same for you! Will you submit to His control and allow Him to shape your convictions?

My 15 Core Convictions

1. I believe that Jesus Christ is the Way, the Truth, and the Life. He was God manifested in flesh and is the only hope of the world.

2. I believe that God has revealed Himself as Father, Son, and Holy Spirit; that in Jesus dwells all the fullness of the Godhead bodily; and that in Him are hidden all the treasures of wisdom and knowledge.

3. I believe that the Bible from Genesis to Revelation is the actual Word of God. Its truths are worth diligently studying, accurately teaching, and doggedly defending. To doggedly defend the truth, however, does not give us license to spew venom on our opponents, for we must always "speak the truth in love."

4. I believe that all Christians are commissioned to share the gospel and to be ready always to give an answer for the hope that is within us, and to do so with humility and godly fear (not arrogance and antagonism).

5. I believe that Christian leaders are called to equip all believers to minister in order to fulfill the great commission and the great commandment.

6. I believe that God is the perfect balance of absolute love and absolute justice; therefore, the accurate proclamation of the gospel will reveal the true nature of God.

7. I believe the proclamation of the gospel includes the death,

burial, resurrection and appearances of Jesus Christ as evidence of who He is. I Cor. 15:1-11. It is also necessary with proper timing to share how to respond to the gospel in faith, repentance, confession and baptism. "For with the heart one believes unto righteousness, and with the mouth confession is made unto salvation." Romans 10:10. "Repent, and let every one of you be baptized in the name of Jesus Christ for the remission of sins; and you shall receive the gift of the Holy Spirit." Acts 2:38. We are saved by grace through faith, not by our good works, for our own best works are filthy rags next to God's righteousness. We are created in Christ Jesus unto good works (the result of our salvation). *"For by grace you have been saved through faith, and that not of yourselves; it is the gift of God, not of works, lest anyone should boast. For we are His workmanship, created in Christ Jesus for good works, which God prepared beforehand that we should walk in them."* Eph. 2:8-10. Genuine trust in Jesus Christ as our sacrifice payment for sin (Savior) is the **essence** of our salvation; the good works that flow out of this trust relationship with Jesus are the evidence of our salvation. **If our trust is in anything or anyone other than Jesus Himself – it is a false, misplaced trust – there is no salvation in it!** *"Nor is there salvation in any other, for there is no other name under heaven given among men by which we must be saved."* Acts 4:12

8. I believe that the key to proclaiming the good news to non-Christian and post-Christian cultures is creation evangelism, i.e. we must begin with God as Almighty Creator to declare Him as Adequate Redeemer as Paul did at Mars Hill. See Acts 17 and Colossians 1:13-22 (which shows that His role as Creator is essential to His role as Redeemer and as Resurrected Lord).

9. I believe that we of the Restoration Movement are Christians only, but we are not the only Christians. We should not alienate other believers by acting like we consider ourselves the only Christians.

10. **I believe that every person on earth is valuable to God and is worth saving.** This of necessity includes enemies of the gospel like hostile editors, evolution devotees, abortion doctors, Marxist professors, Muslim terrorists, pimps and pornographers. We are to be wise in the way we treat outsiders. **We must remember that our real enemy is Satan and that the love-filled apostle Paul was the hate-filled Saul of Tarsus before his conversion.** *"Walk in wisdom toward those who are outside, redeeming the time. Let your speech always be with grace, seasoned with salt, that you may know how you ought to answer each one."* Colossians 4:5-6

11. **I believe that prayer is our first and most dynamic strategy in breaking down Satan's strongholds.** Prayer is not the only thing we are called to do, but until we have prayed and waited on God for direction, we are foolish to charge ahead on our own. **Prayer should always be our first resource rather than our last resort.** *"Continue earnestly in prayer, being vigilant in it with thanksgiving;"* Colossians 4:2

12. I believe that after prayer, love is our most powerful weapon to melt cold hearts and open closed doors. I believe that the New Covenant pivots on two commandments--faith which works by love! Gal. 5:6

13. I believe that Jesus' prayer in John 17:20-21 teaches us that unity in the Body of Christ is the most vital factor in reaching the world for Jesus. The world doesn't need us to teach them how to fight—that is one thing they are really good at. The world needs to look to God's church with longing eyes and say, **"Behold how they love one another."**

14. I believe that we cannot promote Christian unity by compromising God's truth, for in the same high priestly prayer Jesus said *"Sanctify them in thy truth. Thy Word is truth!"* (John 17:17). In our culture, the only virtue is tolerance. The ungodly wisdom

of this world is pressuring us to conform and fit into its mold by tolerating the intolerable. To faithfully follow Jesus means having the backbone to oppose evil. Was Jesus always gentle and mild? Apparently, the money changers in the temple, as well as the Pharisees and the chief priests didn't think so. Jesus Himself said, "If they have hated Me, they will hate you." We must be willing to be misunderstood, hated and slandered for Jesus' sake.

15. Therefore, I believe that to effectively evangelize our lost, confused, hostile world we must carefully balance and prayerfully walk the tightrope stretched between truth and unity. "Lord, fill us with Your Spirit, for we cannot accomplish this on our own."

I Wonder! I Wonder!

Have you ever seen the picture of a small child with a puzzled look and a cloud above him containing the words, "I Wonder! I Wonder!"? I am not the child in that picture, but I could have been, and I relate to him very well. As I consider the amazing, vast implications of the truths contained in Genesis 1:27-28, I wonder! I wonder! Let's look at those verses again. *"So God created man in His own image; in the image of God He created him; male and female He created them. Then God blessed them, and God said to them, 'Be fruitful and multiply; fill the earth and subdue it; have dominion over the fish of the sea, over the birds of the air, and over every living thing that moves on the earth.'"*

I wonder if the Spirit of God inspired both Matthew and Mark to quote Genesis 1:27, not only to show how Jesus quoted this passage to refute the Pharisees when they attempted to trap Him concerning divorce, but also to refute the compromising false doctrines of theistic evolutionism and "progressive creationism." Both of these deviant doctrines teach that millions of years after the original creation of heaven and earth, God "created" Adam and Eve through a progressive process of evolution – yet Jesus Himself said, *"But from the beginning of the creation, God made them male and female"* Mark 10:6. Have you not read that He who made them at the beginning made them male and female" Matthew 19:4. Is it not obvious that Jesus was pointing the Pharisees back to creation week when He made human beings as male and female? **Any form of evolutionism undermines the Word of God and enhances the confusion caused by sin and rebellion. God is not the author of confusion! Jesus spoke clarity – not confusion!**

Have you ever wondered how much more confused an evolutionist could be than to declare that he rejects the supernatural and does not believe in miracles, yet has the audacity to believe that "natural selection" coupled with time and chance work fantastic miracles? Isn't it amazing that from a spark of life that just happened (even though life comes only from life according to scientific studies), thousands upon thousands of creatures evolved simultaneously as a male and a female in each category of creature in order to reproduce? How did they survive and reproduce before their reproductive organs evolved? I wonder! I wonder – how much more gullible can we be than to believe evolutionism and reject the living Word of God? The reproductive system of a male and the corresponding reproductive system of a female of the same kind are intricately designed systems – yet they just happened simultaneously by "chance" without a Designer, without design? Amazing! Simply amazing!

By inspiration, Solomon wrote of the wonder of the way of a man with a maid. Have you ever pondered with wonder and awe the thrill of romance, love, marriage and family as God's gift to those He created in His own image? Have you wondered why the Spirit of God portrays His people, the church, as the Bride of Christ? Will not the wonder of our relationship with Jesus the Bridegroom, exceed the thrill of all earthly relationships?

Do you realize that the wonder of holding their little child, formed as a blend of their own image, is often the spark of inspiration that draws a young couple to seek a church where they can come together with others to worship the Creator?

Have you ever wondered how our Father feels about the ignorance and insolence of those who rebel against His marvelous creation of male and female? Those who think that they know better than the Genius who designed them which they should be – male or female? How does He feel about those who misuse and pervert their sexuality for their own pleasure and destroy their own offspring by abortion? Those who reject the commitment of marriage as the union of one man to one woman for as long as they both shall live, and instead choose recreational sex with one partner after another, expecting to have no responsibility for their actions and no negative repercussions? "Oh, well – we just got here by random chance processes, so we have no Creator to answer to for all this!" Oh, really? Why not just write your own book and name it *Gullible's Travels*?

Excuses

How far will our flimsy excuses for sin and disobedience get us when we stand before the all-knowing Judge of the universe? Consider this passage: *"For the word of God is living and powerful, and sharper than any two-edged sword, piercing even to the division of soul and spirit, and of joints and marrow, and is a discerner of the thoughts and intents of the heart. And there is no creature hidden from His sight, but all things are naked and open to the eyes of Him to whom we must give account."* Hebrews 4:12-13

Will the Judge pretend to be a doting grandfather who says, "Oh, you poor thing," when He hears the excuse, "I just can't help it – I'm hot-blooded like my dad (brother)," etc.? Or the excuses, "I'm a man trapped in a woman's body!" or "I'm a woman trapped in a man's body!" Will He just overlook or wink at the sins of lust, covetousness, ingratitude, whining and griping about what He didn't give me (such as the body parts of the opposite sex). Here are some potent portions of Scripture to ponder:

"The heart is deceitful above all things, and desperately wicked;

who can know it? I, the Lord, search the heart, I test the mind, even to give every man according to his ways, according to the fruit of his doings." Jeremiah 17:9-10

"What shall we say then? Is the law sin? Certainly not! On the contrary, I would not have known sin except through the law. For I would not have known covetousness unless the law had said, 'You shall not covet.' But sin, taking opportunity by the commandment, produced in me all manner of evil desire. For apart from the law sin was dead." Romans 7:7-8 Coveting is lusting after something you don't have but someone else has.

*"**But godliness with contentment is great gain,** for we brought nothing into the world, and we cannot take anything out of the world. But if we have food and clothing, with these we will be content. But those who desire to be rich fall into temptation, into a snare, into many senseless and harmful desires that plunge people into ruin and destruction."* 1 Timothy 6:6-9 (ESV)

*"**Blessed is the man who endures temptation;** for when he has been approved, he will receive the crown of life which the Lord has promised to those who love Him. Let no one say when he is tempted, 'I am tempted by God'; for God cannot be tempted by evil, nor does He Himself tempt anyone. But each one is tempted when he is drawn away by his own desires and enticed. Then, when desire has conceived, it gives birth to sin; and sin, when it is full-grown, brings forth death. Do not be deceived, my beloved brethren. Every good gift and every perfect gift is from above, and comes down from the Father of lights, with whom there is no variation or shadow of turning. Of His own will He brought us forth by the word of truth, that we might be a kind of firstfruits of His creatures."* James 1:12-18

If we think we can get by with our miserable excuses, we better think again. How well did that work for Adam and Eve? Our Father initiated the punishment He had warned and promised them, and we are still seeing the horrible multiplied consequences of living on this cursed earth, which has become a veil of tears, suffering and death.

Our Father is the epitome of integrity! He says what He means, and He means what He says!

Excuses? NO! Deep repentance coupled with confessing and forsaking sin – now that is another matter entirely! *"And if you call on the Father, who without partiality judges according to each one's work, conduct yourselves throughout the time of your stay here in fear; knowing that you were not redeemed with corruptible things, like silver or gold, from your aimless conduct received by tradition from your fathers, but with the precious blood of Christ, as of a lamb without blemish and without spot."* 1 Peter 1:17-19

I've heard a preacher on the radio say repeatedly, "God is not mad at you!" Oh, really? Has he never read this passage: **"God is a just judge, and God is angry with the wicked every day. ...** *Behold, the wicked brings forth iniquity; yes, he conceives trouble and brings forth falsehood. He made a pit and dug it out, and has fallen into the ditch which he made. "His trouble shall return upon his own head, and his violent dealing shall come down on his own crown."* Psalm 7:11, 14-16. What about this one: *"For the wrath of God is revealed from heaven against all ungodliness and unrighteousness of men, who suppress the truth in unrighteousness, because what may be known of God is manifest in them, for God has shown it to them. For since the creation of the world His invisible attributes are clearly seen, being understood by the things that are made, even His eternal power and Godhead, so that they are without excuse,"* Romans 1:18-20 **Perhaps that preacher should write another book and name it,** *I Was Wrong!* **The fact that "God so loved the world that He gave His only begotten Son, that whoever believes in Him should not perish but have everlasting life" John 3:16, does not mean that He is not angry with our sin. He is our loving Father – and He is angry with our disobedience. Every parent can relate!**

Now please notice what the Holy Spirit inspired Paul to write immediately after "so that they are without excuse,": **"because, although they knew God, they did not glorify *Him* as God, nor** were thankful, but became futile in their thoughts, and their foolish hearts were darkened. Professing to be wise, they became fools," Romans 1:21-22

The sin of ingratitude is an issue that we should not overlook or neglect to consider. The Holy Spirit specifically points to this sin in the rebellious attitude causing the downward spiral of apostasy, idolatry, immorality, perversion and violence described here in Romans 1. Please also notice this passage: "*Therefore, as the Holy Spirit says: 'Today, if you will hear His voice, do not harden your hearts as in the rebellion, in the day of trial in the wilderness, where your fathers tested Me, tried Me, and saw My works forty years. Therefore I was angry with that generation, and said, 'They always go astray in their heart, and they have not known My ways.' So I swore in My wrath, 'They shall not enter My rest.' Beware, brethren, lest there be in any of you an evil heart of unbelief in departing from the living God; but exhort one another daily, while it is called 'Today,' lest any of you be hardened through the deceitfulness of sin. For we have become partakers of Christ if we hold the beginning of our confidence steadfast to the end,*" Hebrews 2:7-14

Almighty God was angry with his rebellious children who saw His works in providing water from a rock to quench their thirst in the wilderness and miraculously provide manna for their food for 40 years, yet would not believe in His goodness and providence to fulfill their needs in the Promised Land. Is there any parent of a teen who has not felt the hurt and sting of ingratitude? The entitlement mentality is a deeply ingrained, sinful habit in human hearts. It began in the Garden of Eden and has continued relentlessly through eons of time. Does it sting and stab the heart of God for a human being to be unthankful for the gender the Creator has given to him or her?

Whiners are not winners with God!

Pressing On

I am so thankful that God delivered me from my pit and put me in His family. I often sit at my desk and look up at the beautiful picture of racing horses with the verse, *"I press on toward the goal to win the prize for which God has called me heavenward in Christ Jesus!"* Philippians 3:14. I ask Him to guide me in how to keep on keeping on pressing toward the goal. I look to my right where I can focus on two pictures of my beautiful bride and thank God for giving me Della as my wife, companion and co-worker for so many years. I look around the room and thank God for giving us our son, our daughter, our grandkids, and our emotionally adopted kids and grandkids. I ask our loving Father to lead every one of them Home to Jesus and enlist them effectively in His service. I feel like the richest man alive, and I thank Him for life, abundant life, eternal life – for peace and joy and purpose and power to live in His will and way. I am most richly blessed, and I wish the same for you. Thank you for reading this – please share it.

Clinching our Convictions

The heart of the problem is always the problem of the heart! Isn't this the reason why Jesus identified the greatest commandment to be, **"Love the Lord your God with all your heart and with all your soul and with all your strength"** Deuteronomy 6:5 (NIV)? Also, Jesus may well have had in mind Proverbs 4:23, **"Above all else, guard your heart, for it is the wellspring of life."** (NIV)

Walking in Love

Now with Jesus' own perspective in clear view, let us consider what the Spirit of Christ wrote to the Ephesian believers about what it means to "walk in love": *"Follow God's example, therefore, as dearly loved children and walk in the way of love, just as Christ loved us and gave himself up for us as a fragrant offering and sacrifice to God. But among you there must not be even a hint of sexual immorality, or of any kind of impurity, or of greed, because these are improper for God's holy people. Nor should there be obscenity, foolish talk or coarse joking, which are out of place, but rather thanksgiving. For of this you can be sure: No immoral, impure or greedy person—such a person is an idolater—has any inheritance in the kingdom of Christ and of God. Let no one deceive you with empty words, for because of such things God's wrath comes on those who are disobedient. Therefore do not be partners with them."* Ephesians 5:1-7 (NIV)

Does this passage have relevance to a man who is dissatisfied with the male body parts that God has given him? (This may very well extend to every last cell of his body that is male instead of female.) Since the word covet means to strongly desire something that belongs to someone else, why would this passage not apply to a man who strongly desires female body parts which God did not give him? He may even be willing to go through "hormone therapy" and invasive surgery to get what he wants, and may end up even more dissatisfied than before. Remember, the heart of the problem is always the problem of the heart! Can he disregard and disobey God's command to be content with what he has instead of coveting what other people have and not suffer severe consequences?

Now let's look at verses 5-7 again, this time from the (NKJV): *"For this you know, that no fornicator, unclean person, **nor covetous man, who is an idolater,** has any inheritance in the kingdom of Christ and God. Let no one deceive you with empty words, for because of these things the wrath of God comes upon the sons of disobedience. Therefore do not be partakers with them."*

Have you Heard about "Gay" Christians?

If by this question you mean those who are practicing sodomy while professing to be Christians and are unrepentant, the Word of God in Ephesians is very clear. The Spirit of God also made it clear to the believers in Corinth (a notorious sin-city): *"Do you not know that the unrighteous will not inherit the kingdom of God? Do not be deceived. Neither fornicators, nor idolaters, nor adulterers, nor homosexuals, nor sodomites, nor thieves, nor covetous, nor drunkards, nor revilers, nor extortioners will inherit the kingdom of God. And such were some of you. But you were washed, but you were sanctified, but you were justified in the name of the Lord Jesus and by the Spirit of our God."* 1 Corinthians 6:9-11

As Christians, we are to be identified with Christ by a new nature being transformed into His likeness, not by the old nature that identified us in the flesh! **We are converts and if we have not been converted, we are not Christians no matter what we may profess.**

To the Romans Paul wrote: *"What shall we say then? Shall we continue in sin that grace may abound? Certainly not!* **How shall we who died to sin live any longer in it?** *Or do you not know that as many of us as were baptized into Christ Jesus were baptized into His death? Therefore we were buried with Him through baptism into death, that just as Christ was raised from the dead by the glory of the Father, even so we also should walk in newness of life."* Romans 6:1-4

The apostle John wrote: ***"Now by this we know that we know Him, if we keep His commandments.*** *He who says, 'I know Him,' and does not keep His commandments, is a liar, and the truth is not in him. But whoever keeps His word, truly the love of God is perfected in him. By this we know that we are in Him. He who says he abides in Him ought himself also to walk just as He walked. ...Do not love the world or the things in the world. If anyone loves the world, the love of the Father is not in him. For all that is in the world—the lust of the flesh, the lust of the eyes, and the pride of life—is not of the Father but is of the world. And the world is passing away, and the lust of it; but he who does the will of God abides forever."* 1 John 2:3-6, 15-17

Transfixed and Transformed

"Now the Lord is the Spirit; and where the Spirit of the Lord is, there is liberty. But we all, with unveiled face, beholding as in a mirror the glory of the Lord, are being transformed into the same image from glory to glory, just as by the Spirit of the Lord. ...For though we walk in the flesh, we do not war according to the flesh. For the weapons of our warfare are not carnal but mighty in God for pulling down strongholds,

casting down arguments and every high thing that exalts itself against the knowledge of God, **bringing every thought into captivity to the obedience of Christ,**" 2 Corinthians 3:17-18; 10:3-5

Facing Reality

The reality is that we live on a cursed earth because of the rebellion of our original parents and the severe consequences that followed – sickness, suffering and death. One of the severe consequences is that every one of us descendants of that rebellious couple inherits a rebellious nature that is attracted to sin like metal to a magnet.

Back to Nature?

For many years there has been a back-to-nature movement in America, and around the world. The underlying false assumption is that if it is natural, it's good for us. This false assumption is connected with other false assumptions, including evolutionism, environmentalism, and nudist colonies. Is it true "that if it is natural, it's good for us"? It is true that natural supplements are often much better for us than prescription drugs – however, it is also true that poison oak, poison ivy, marijuana, and a skunk's protective system are natural!

When I was a young boy, a catchy tune that rose to popularity on music charts and TV programs was "Doin' What Comes Naturally." It was based on the assumption that natural is good – but it probably helped pave the way for the sexual revolution of the 1960's along with the lie of "free love." Does God have anything to say to us about worshiping nature and giving ourselves over to "doin' what comes naturally"? Yes! Definitely! Here it is: *"For the wrath of God is revealed from heaven against all ungodliness and unrighteousness of men, who suppress the truth in unrighteousness, because what may be known of God is manifest in them, for God has shown it to them. For since the creation of the world His invisible attributes are clearly seen, being understood by the things that are made, even His eternal power and Godhead, so* *that they are without excuse, because, although they knew God, they did not glorify Him as God, nor were thankful, but became futile in their thoughts, and their **foolish hearts were darkened**. Professing to be wise, they became fools, and changed the glory of the incorruptible God into an image made like corruptible man—and birds and four-footed animals and creeping things. Therefore God also gave them up to uncleanness, in the lusts of their hearts, to dishonor their bodies among themselves, who exchanged the truth of God for the lie, and worshiped and served the creature rather than the Creator, who is blessed forever. Amen. For this reason God gave them up to vile passions. For even their women exchanged the natural use for what is against nature. Likewise also the men, leaving the natural use of the woman, burned in their lust for one another, men with men committing what is shameful, and receiving in themselves the penalty of their error which was due. And even as they did not like to retain God in their knowledge, God gave them over to a debased mind, to do those things which are not fitting; being filled with all unrighteousness, sexual immorality, wickedness, covetousness, maliciousness; full of envy, murder, strife, deceit, evil-mindedness; they are whisperers, backbiters, haters of God, violent, proud, boasters, inventors of evil things, disobedient to parents, undiscerning, untrustworthy, unloving, unforgiving, unmerciful; who, knowing the righteous judgment of God, that those who practice such things are deserving of death, not only do the same but also approve of those who practice them.”* Romans 1:18-32

Darkened! Degenerate! Depraved!

Human beings, in our fallen nature, are naturally attracted to the idolatry of worshiping the creature and the sensuality of pursuing sexual pleasure without responsibility. However, the sensuality can and often does degenerate into depravity (perversions that are against nature). The degeneration continues into every form of evil imaginable.

Did reading this portion of Scripture open your eyes to what has happened to our once great nation? Are you on board with "Make America Great Again!"?

Are Christians Hypocrites?

Have you read the discouraging statistics from George Barna which indicate that most professing Christians in America are watching the same junk and living the same immoral lives as non-Christians? In view of these revealing statistics, we need to ask ourselves (and others) some probing questions. Here are a few:

1. Is there a difference between professing Christians and genuine Christians?

2. Is there a difference between true religion and false religion? Consider: *"If anyone among you thinks he is religious, and does not bridle his tongue but deceives his own heart, this one's religion is useless. Pure and undefiled religion before God and the Father is this: to visit orphans and widows in their trouble, and to keep oneself unspotted from the world."* James 1:26-17

3. Is there a difference between "baby Christians" (new converts with worldly habits) and mature Christians?

4. Will we ever become so mature as Christians still living on this cursed earth that we never sin anymore (not even a harsh word to an offender)? The Holy Spirit inspired James to write: *"My brethren, let not many of you become teachers, knowing that we shall receive a stricter judgment. For we all stumble in many things. If anyone does not stumble in word, he is a perfect man, able also to bridle the whole body."* James 3:1-2

5. Aren't all of us tempted to hide our faults and exaggerate our virtues in order to impress others? (Think of Facebook, interviews, shop talk, fish stories, dating services, etc.)

6. Is there no such thing as cultural hypocrisy among non-Christians? Is there no one in bar rooms telling tall tales and pretending

to be someone or something that he (or she) is not? Consider these pertinent questions from Ravi Zacharias:

"How is it that the conscience of a people that pleads for the protection of the children of illegal caravans coming into the country can also argue for the death of American children even when they are just newborn? Children are the weakest in our midst. How can some be defendable -and the others be expendable?" (Quoted from Ravi Zacharias in the RZIM June 11, 2019 newsletter)

7. Critic, are you examining your own heart yet? Do you need to repent, ask forgiveness, and submit your life to the control of our Lord Jesus Christ?

So, are Christians hypocrites? In some cases, yes! And in those cases, the perpetrators need to repent, like Peter did after denying that he even knew Jesus.

There are many who claim to be Christians but are not at all Christians according to God's Word. Then there are the strugglers, who want to do right but keep falling back into sinful old habits. See Romans 7.

With Whom Will You Walk?

by Joe Garman

"I heard of an incident that shows the power of God even among the gangs in prison. The chaplain of a maximum security prison preached a Sunday morning sermon that converted a notorious gang member. The inmate accepted Christ and surrendered his 'patch of gang affiliation' to the chaplain. Some of the inmates became concerned about his safety.

Correctional Officers were also worried about the potential fallout. He was confident he had made the right decision, but was transferred to solitary confinement for protection. Meanwhile, the leader of the gang called an emergency meeting. Later, a message was sent to the new believer telling him what they decided. **'Walk the walk and talk the talk and you will be safe!'**

No threats …no retaliation. You never know when or where the Word of God will land, but we can rest assured it does not return to Him void. Give praise to God that not only was a man convicted of his sin but even those who did not have His faith, respected God enough to leave His anointed alone. The Lord of the chapel was also the Lord of the solitary confinement cell. (Joe Garman, American Rehabilitation Ministries)

Temptation! Truth! Triumph!

For those who have repented but are struggling with the temptations of their old lifestyles here are pertinent passages: *"This is the message which we have heard from Him and declare to you, that God is light and in Him is no darkness at all. If we say that we have fellowship with Him, and walk in darkness, we lie and do not practice the truth. But if we walk in the light as He is in the light, we have fellowship with one another, and* **the blood of Jesus Christ His Son cleanses us from all sin.** *If we say that we have no sin, we deceive ourselves, and the truth is not in us. If we confess our sins, He is faithful and just to forgive us our sins and to cleanse us from all unrighteousness."* 1 John 1:5-9 **"No temptation has overtaken you except such as is common to man; but God is faithful, who will not allow you to be tempted beyond what you are able, but with the temptation will also make the way of escape, that you may be able to bear it.** *… Therefore, whether you eat or drink, or whatever you do, do all to the glory of God."* 1 Corinthians 10:13, 31

Keep Your Heart!

As we consider the saying, "The heart of the problem is always the problem of the heart!" can we be certain that it is a true statement? In view of Proverbs 4:23, I believe that the answer is definitely, yes! In the NKJV it is translated: *"Keep your heart with all diligence, for out of it spring the issues of life."* In the NLV it is translated: *"Keep your heart pure for out of it are the important things of life."*

For final confirmation in Scripture of this vital truth, please look with me at Jeremiah 17:9-10: *"The heart is deceitful above all things, and desperately sick; who can understand it? 'I the Lord search the heart and test the mind, to give every man according to his ways, according to the fruit of his deeds'"* (ESV). Does this confirm the important truth that the heart of the problem is always the problem of the heart? Definitely! Powerfully! Now in view of this Biblical confirmation about the heart of the problem, here are a few probing questions:

1. Where does the Word of God excuse murder on the basis of insanity?

2. Is there any excuse for any other crime on the basis of insanity given in Scripture?

3. Wasn't Satan's rebellion against the eternal, all-powerful, all-knowing God the epitome of insanity?

4. Did God excuse Adam and Eve for their rebellion because she was deceived by the original insane liar?

5. Did our wise Father excuse Adam because he was not deceived, but rather chose to sin with Eve rather than to stand alone for God?

6. Wasn't Adam's sin, therefore, the first case of idolatry (making Eve more important to himself than God)?

7. Is there any excuse in Scripture for the practice of sodomy?

8. Is there any excuse in the Word of God for transgender practices?

9. Since human beings, even when still very small children, are capable of deceiving themselves as well as others – should we not be constantly on guard about being deceived? (In prison ministry I learned to become very cautious because prisoners can be so convincing that they are innocent and that it was all someone else's fault. And small kids can be expert con-artists and manipulators to bring others to see it their way!)

10. Should we be more receptive to the compassionate speculations of psychologists about sodomy and transgender issues than we are to the strong and clear teachings of the Word of God? Haven't most Christian psychologists already compromised many of the clear teachings of the Word of God in adopting the humanistic speculations of the founders of the various branches of the very subjective "science" of psychology? (Freud, Jung, and Rogers to name a few among many.) Hmmm!

11. Where does the Word of God show us any exception to the sanctity of sexuality or Biblical morality for any reason – including "gender identity"?

12. Is the Word of God actually our final word of authority, or should we compromise for convenience and "compassion"?

13. Is it true that when we compromise on convictions, we become part of the problem we once sought to solve?

14. Does is also seem ironic to you that the plea for compassion by homosexuals since at least the 1980's has been, "I was born that way!" but now the plea for those in the LGBTQ movement who desire to be trans-sexual is, "I was born in the wrong body!" Could it be that the root of each plea is more propaganda than truth? Con artists can come across as very convincing. (Isn't that where "con" comes from in the term "con- artist"?)

Examination Station

If you are portraying yourself as a "gay Christian" while continuing to practice the sin of sodomy, or if you are dissatisfied with the body parts that God has graciously given you, and you are an ungrateful complainer who is coveting the body parts God has not given you (male or female), please be honest enough to carefully and prayerfully examine these powerful portions of God's Word: *"Who can understand his errors? Cleanse me from secret faults. Keep back Your servant also from presumptuous sins; let them not have dominion over me. Then*

I shall be blameless, and I shall be innocent of great transgression. Let the words of my mouth and the meditation of my heart be acceptable in Your sight, O Lord, my strength and my Redeemer." Psalm 19:12-14; *"Examine me, O Lord, and prove me; try my mind and my heart."* Psalm 26:2; *"The heart is deceitful above all things, and desperately wicked; who can know it? I, the Lord, search the heart, I test the mind, even to give every man according to his ways, according to the fruit of his doings."* Jeremiah 17:9-10; *"Is it not from the mouth of the Most High that woe and well-being proceed? Why should a living man complain, a man for the punishment of his sins? Let us search out and examine our ways, and turn back to the Lord; let us lift our hearts and hands to God in heaven. We have transgressed and rebelled; You have not pardoned."* Lamentations 3:38-42; *"For I received from the Lord that which I also delivered to you: that the Lord Jesus on the same night in which He was betrayed took bread; and when He had given thanks, He broke it and said, 'Take, eat; this is My body which is broken for you; do this in remembrance of Me.' In the same manner He also took the cup after supper, saying, 'This cup is the new covenant in My blood. This do, as often as you drink it, in remembrance of Me.' For as often as you eat this bread and drink this cup, you proclaim the Lord's death till He comes. Therefore whoever eats this bread or drinks this cup of the Lord in an unworthy manner will be guilty of the body and blood of the Lord. But let a man examine himself, and so let him eat of the bread and drink of the cup. For he who eats and drinks in an unworthy manner eats and drinks judgment to himself, not discerning the Lord's body."* 1 Corinthians 11:23-29; *"Examine yourselves as to whether you are in the faith. Test yourselves. Do you not know yourselves, that Jesus Christ is in you?—unless indeed you are disqualified."* 2 Corinthians 13:5

Processing Priorities

If you will open your Bible and read the last half of Romans 1 again, you will find a clear and vivid portrayal of what has been happening to our country because of the infiltration of godless humanism (atheism) into our educational system in the 20th and 21st centuries. To understand this infiltration even better, you may want to study the purposes and tactics of Horace Mann and John Dewey. "The mess we's in" is the result of careful design and infiltration – not random chance processes.

However, what has happened and is happening did not catch God off guard! He is the all-knowing Genius who created us and who has also warned us. His ultimate plan and purpose will not be derailed by the puny plans and purposes of pontificating "progressives"!

Here is the warning:

Perilous Times Propagated and Promoted by "Progressives"

**(Their perspective of progress is plunging
us into the pit of perversions!)**

"But know this, that in the last days perilous times will come: for men will be lovers of themselves, lovers of money, boasters, proud, blasphemers, disobedient to parents, unthankful, unholy, unloving, unforgiving, slanderers, without self-control, brutal, despisers of good, traitors, headstrong, haughty, lovers of pleasure rather than lovers of God, having a form of godliness but denying its power. And from such people turn away!" 2 Timothy 3:1-5

Here is God's Purpose – Which Cannot be Thwarted!

"To me, who am less than the least of all the saints, this grace was given, that I should preach among the Gentiles the unsearchable riches of Christ, and to make all see what is the fellowship of the mystery, which from the beginning of the ages has been hidden in God who created all things through Jesus Christ; to the intent that now the manifold wisdom of God might be made known by the church to the principalities and powers in the heavenly places, according to the eternal purpose which He accomplished in Christ Jesus our Lord, in whom we have boldness and access with confidence through faith in Him." Ephesians 3:8-12

What Shall We Do?

What God told Solomon, and through him, all of ancient Israel about what to do about the devastation that would come because of ignoring their Creator and rebelling against His Word is still true and valid for Christians in the 21st century. *"if My people who are called by My name will humble themselves, and pray and seek My face, and turn from their wicked ways, then I will hear from heaven, and will forgive their sin and heal their land."* 2 Chronicles 7:14

"God, Give Us Men..."

"God give us men...ribbed with the steel of Your Holy Spirit...men who will not flinch when the battle's fiercest...men who won't acquiesce, or compromise, or fade when the enemy rages. God give us men who can't be bought, bartered, or badgered by the enemy, men who will pay the price, make the sacrifice, stand the ground, and hold the torch high. God give us men obsessed with the principles true to your Word, men stripped of self-seeking and a yen for security...men who will pay any price for freedom and go any lengths for truth. God give us men delivered from mediocrity, men with vision high, pride low, faith wide, love deep, and patience long...men who will dare to march to the drumbeat of a distant drummer, men who will not surrender principles of truth in order to accommodate their peers. God give us men more interested in scars than medals. More committed to conviction than convenience, men who will give their life for the eternal, instead of indulging their lives for a moment in time. Give us men who are fearless in the face of danger, calm in the midst of pressure, bold in the midst of opposition. God give us men who will pray earnestly, work long, preach clearly, and wait patiently. Give us men whose walk is by faith, behavior is by principle, whose dreams are in heaven, and whose book is the Bible. God give us men who are equal to the task. These are the men the church needs today." (The Growth Factor, Bob Moorehead)

"Fellowship of the Unashamed"

"I am part of the 'Fellowship of the Unashamed.' The die has been cast. I have stepped over the line. The decision has been made. I am a disciple of Jesus Christ. I won't look back, go back, hold back, let up, slow down, back away, hesitate or be still. My past is redeemed, my present remade, and my future re-aimed. I am finished and done with low living, sight walking, small planning, smooth knees, colorless dreams, chintzy giving, and dwarfed goals.

I no longer need preeminence, prosperity, position, promotions, plaudits, or popularity. I now live by presence, lean by faith, love by patience, lift by prayer, and labor by power. My pace is set, my gait is fast, my goal is Heaven, my road is narrow, my way is rough, my companions few, my Guide reliable, my mission clear. I cannot be bought, compromised, deterred, lured away, turned back, diluted, or delayed.

I will not flinch in the face of sacrifice, hesitate in the presence of adversity, negotiate at the table of the enemy, ponder at the pool of popularity or meander in the maze of mediocrity. I am a disciple of Jesus Christ. I must go until Heaven returns, give until I drop, preach until all know, and work until He comes. And when He comes to get His own, He will have no problem recognizing me. My colors will be clear." (The Author of this work is a Rwandan man in 1980 who was forced by his tribe to either renounce Christ or face certain death. He refused to renounce Christ, and he was killed on the spot. The night before he had written the commitment "The Fellowship of the Unashamed" which was found in his room. Bob Moorehead had written this in his book "Worlds Aptly Spoken" c. 1995)

Christ-Confident – Not Self-Confident!

Any man who chooses to answer the call, "God give us men," and anyone who enlists in the "Fellowship of the Unashamed" will become a prime target for Satan's devises, deceptions and darts! So, when you step up, be prepared for warfare, be prayed up, be equipped and be dependent! Totally dependent on the Spirit of God and the power of God – not your own strength or resolve. Here are very important passages for preparations:

"Look carefully then how you walk, not as unwise but as wise, making the best use of the time, because the days are evil. Therefore do not be foolish, but understand what the will of the Lord is. And do not get drunk with wine, for that is debauchery, but be filled with the Spirit," Ephesians 5:15-18 (ESV). *"Finally, be strong in the Lord and in the strength of his might. Put on the whole armor of God, that you may be able to stand against the schemes of the devil. For we do not wrestle against flesh and blood, but against the rulers, against the authorities, against the cosmic powers over this present darkness, against the spiritual forces of evil in the heavenly places. Therefore take up the whole armor of God, that you may be able to withstand in the evil day, and having done all, to stand firm. Stand therefore, having fastened on the belt of truth, and having put on the breastplate of righteousness, and, as shoes for your feet, having put on the readiness given by the gospel of peace. In all circumstances take up the shield of faith, with which you can extinguish all the flaming darts of the evil one; and take the helmet of salvation, and the sword of the Spirit, which is the word of God, praying at all times in the Spirit, with all prayer and supplication. To that end, keep alert with all perseverance, making supplication for all the saints,"* Ephesians 6:10-18 (ESV)

Do you feel that the hound of heaven is on your trail, relentlessly pursuing you to rescue you from yourself, your selfish habits, your pet sins and your satanic delusions? If so, it's high time to thank Him, repent, and surrender your life, your heart and your soul to the Lord Jesus Christ. The fact that He is still pursuing you is encouraging. He hasn't given up on you – yet! There is a point of no return. Consider this insightful message by Henry M. Morris III, in Days of Praise for Friday, September 13, 2019:

"The Point of No Return"

"The leaders of Ephraim (a collective term for the 10 northern tribes of Israel) had passed this point of no return They had become completely infatuated with the pantheistic polytheism of the nations, being 'joined' to their symbolic models of natural forces and all the immoral practices that accompanied such nature worship. The word for 'joined' means 'fascinated by.' They had been brought so deeply under the occult powers behind these nature-god idols as to be irrevocably committed to them, so that it would be a waste of time and tears to try to reclaim them now.

The Scriptures contain many similar warnings. 'My spirit shall not always strive with man' (Genesis 6:3). 'Let them alone: they be blind leaders of the blind' (Matthew 15:14). 'There is a sin unto death: I do not say that he shall pray for it' (1 John 5:16). 'Give not that which is holy unto the dogs, neither cast ye your pearls before swine' (Mathew 7:6). Pharaoh repeatedly 'hardened his heart' against God, and finally God Himself hardened Pharaoh's heart (e.g., Exodus 8:15; 10:27). 'God gave them up' (Romans 1:24, 26,28).

These should be sobering words to anyone who is becoming enchanted with evolutionism, or occultism, or any form of pantheistic humanism. As long as such a person has any qualm of conscience, or even any doubts about the pseudo-scientific philosophy to which he his becoming addicted, there is hope that he might yet turn to the true God of creation. To continue in his present course, however, is presumptuous and deadly. The time will come, perhaps sooner than he thinks, when God will say: 'Let him alone.'" HMM. Used by permission. (© 1994-2019 Institute for Creation Research. All Rights Reserved. www.icr.org)

It's Now or Never!

For years I warned my students of this song because it has a hauntingly beautiful melody with a dangerous message. I told them that this is not a song about love - it's a song about lust! With the lyrics that Elvis made popular, that was the case, but our friend, Rick Rodriguez, changed that song for us. Rick was a master musician who started his own Christian band, Double-Edged Sword, and he learned from another Christian band, A Band of Brothers, how to take a popular melody and "convert" it with Christian lyrics. Rick converted "It's Now or Never" into a strong evangelistic appeal. Consider these words:

"It's now or never - come hold Him tight.
Reach out to Jesus - reach out tonight.
Tomorrow may be too late;
God's waiting for you -
Don't hesitate!

When your soul is aching,
And your heart is breaking,
And you feel like crying,
Even feel like dying -

Just call to the Father;
It won't be a bother.
He's there for you
To see you through - tonight.

It's now or never - come hold Him tight.
Reach out to heaven - reach out tonight.
Tomorrow may be too late;
God's waiting for you -
Don't hesitate!"

Rick Rodriguez was born the same year I was - just a few months ahead of me - and I attended his memorial service in Nampa a few years ago. What a powerful testimony of a changed life! One person after another testified to Rick's positive impact on his or her life. The fact that Rick Rodriguez was only months older than I am, reminded me how fleeting life on this earth is - and I want to make my life count day by day and moment by moment. How about you? What are you doing today to touch someone else with the truth and love of Jesus? Are you ready to stand before Him as your Judge? He died to be your

Savior. Have you reached out to Him? Tomorrow may be too late! (Lyrics to the song used by permission of Rick's wife, Joyce.)

Where Was God on 9/11?

Today, as I write this, it is September 11, 2019 – 18 years since the terrible attacks by suicide terrorists that killed nearly 3,000 people. I still vividly remember receiving an email note of empathy from Vlad Devakov expressing his sorrow over this tragedy and telling us that his tears were dropping onto his keyboard as he typed the message. Vlad was my first interpreter for the Man and the Christian Worldview Symposium in May 2001. Today, tears will be flowing from millions of eyes for those who were murdered that day, for the first responders' who sacrificed their lives or their health to rescue people trapped in the towers, the Pentagon or the plane, plus those grieving over the recent Taliban attacks in Afghanistan, the fatalities and injuries from mass shootings, fires, floods, hurricanes, tornadoes, accidents, etc.

On 9/11, many people were asking Christian leaders, "Why?" or "Where is God now?" Some had no answer, but some had good answers based on a Biblical Christian Worldview. Why? Because we are living on a cursed earth, that's why! Why are we on a cursed earth? Because of sin, that's why! Human rebellion against the rule of Almighty God, the loving Father who created them in His own image as male and female and put them on a perfect earth in a beautiful garden with an abundance of everything they needed. There was only one restriction, which gave Adam and Eve the power of choice (which was part of being created in His own image). Instead of obeying their Father, they chose to fall for Satan's deception, thereby bringing the curse of suffering and death upon earth. Every one of us has made the same kind of foolish, ungodly choices in our own lives.

Where was God on 9/11? The same place He was when corrupted and deluded human beings rejected His only begotten Son, mocked Him, cursed Him, spit on Him, and nailed Him to an old rugged cross! That is where He shed His precious blood to rescue you from your sin – and me from mine. He made forgiveness possible for us. He was the first responder and the **only** responder who could rescue us – because He had no sin! What are we doing with Jesus? Are we sharing His truth and love so others can be rescued? Please pray!

"The Spirit and the Bride say, 'Come.' And let the one who hears say, 'Come.' And let the one who is thirsty come; let the one who desires take the water of life without price. … He who testifies to these things says, 'Surely I am coming soon.' Amen. Come, Lord Jesus! The grace of the Lord Jesus be with all. Amen." Revelation 22:17, 20-21 (ESV)

Questions for Chapter 6

1. What is it about Genesis 1:27 that "is so obvious? Who would question such an obvious truth?"

2. What does Larry Spargimino point out that is "Stranger Than Fiction – But Tragically Real"?

3. What does Larry point out under the heading, "Disappointed by Transitioning"?

4. What was most important to you from the section, "Satan's Devastating War on the Mind"?

5. What is the difference between opinions and convictions and what difference does it make?

6. Of the 15 Core Convictions I shared with you, what two resonate most strongly with you?

7. What resonated most with you about "Keep Your Heart"?

8. Why is the message in "God Give Us Men" important to the purpose of this book, *More than Conquerors in Cultural Clashes*?

9. Why is the message in "Fellowship of the Unashamed" important to the purpose of this book, *More than Conquerors in Cultural Clashes*?

10. Why is the message in "It's Now or Never" important to the purpose of this book, *More than Conquerors in Cultural Clashes*?

Bonus Questions

1. What is the most important thing you have learned, re-learned, or received from reading this book?

2. What are you going to do about it? Plan now – and act on your plan! *"But be doers of the word, and not hearers only, deceiving yourselves. ... But he who looks into the perfect law of liberty and continues in it, and is not a forgetful hearer but a doer of the work, this one will be blessed in what he does."* James 1:22, 25

The Triangle of Triumph

"Rejoice always, pray without ceasing, in everything give thanks; for this is the will of God in Christ Jesus for you." 1 Thessalonians 5:16-18

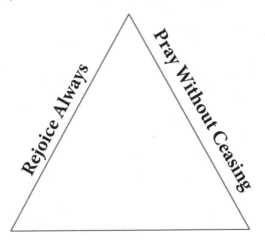

In everything give thanks for this is the will of God in Christ Jesus FOR YOU!

Have you ever gone through a time when you didn't feel like rejoicing? You didn't feel like praying? You didn't feel like thanking? So have I! But then, so what? Are you going to obey your feelings - or obey God?

Do you suppose every firefighter functions on his feelings? Does he always just jump out of bed in the middle of the night when the alarm sounds because he feels like it? Does he rush out to risk his life fighting fires because he feels like it? Or does he move out because he has a commitment? Do we have a commitment to obey God because it's the right thing to do – no matter how we feel at the moment? The wonderful feelings follow obedience! The thrill of seeing God work in our circumstances when we praise Him in the midst of the storm are beyond comparing to any tinsel thrill this world has to offer!

Reviewer Comments

(Note: These reviews were written before this book was published for the first time – in 2013 - during the Obama administration.)

"Rick, I know your heart for the Lord and the lost. I have always had deep admiration for you for your heart and life. I do not find you offensive nor overly blunt. I look forward to reading what you have to say. We do live when the USA is falling apart. I don't know how much longer it can survive, not long I believe with the current direction. Something needs to be done to warn people. I have just been studying the Persian Empire and have observed that there were many similarities with them and the USA. They lasted 200 years and ruled the world. We have lasted just over 200 years and have been the strongest nation in the world's history. But we are now bankrupt financially and morally. I cannot believe what people are willing to accept from our national and state leaders. It is a huge mess...."

(Next paragraph is after he reviewed Chapter 2):

"Rick: This is SUPER great! I find no fault with it, wish it could be widely circulated and read. I did not read it for punctuation and proper English, but for content. As you know, I am very busy at the present, with more work every week than I can accomplish. But in reading it I find it is right on target and conveys in a very clear way my own views. God Bless you and Della.
  Your friend and brother;
  Charles Crane, Eagle Christian Church"

"Rick: I have read Chapter 4 and agree with you and your stand for Biblical morality and against perversion. I am impressed with your knowledge of the subject and ability to state clearly the issues involved. I thank God for your willingness to stand for right and truth....I heartily endorse this excellent work.

Your brother, Charles Crane"

* * * * * * * * *

"This is all great material that is powerful truth as a Christian apologetic! We can pray God will use this to spread His gospel message!"
~ Rich Schell

* * * * * * * * *

"This chapter is a very strongly worded and forceful declaration of what needs to be heard in the USA. I think your wording and message is very appropriate and clear without being condescending. Did not find anything I would suggest you change. The chapter is strongly worded for patriotic presentation, but the message cannot be diluted and be effective.....I very much enjoyed reading your thoughts. Your comments are things I have felt for a long time need to be expressed to America."
~ D. Lloyd Thomas

* * * * * * * * *

"Very good once again. I agree with you completely. Get this published and I pray everyone reads it. I couldn't improve on it at all. Couple minor comments. Page 4: I agree about 'gay'. I hate it that the homosexual community has spoiled a good word that used to mean happy and carefree...Page 5: My pastor says, 'What you compromise to keep, you will lose.'.....

Thanks, Blessings, Stan Brower"

* * * * * * * * * *

"Hi bolder soldier!

"Wow, what a powerful exposé of the enemy's strategy. It's hard to imagine how far our country has moved from her 'roots'! From the president on down, we are being pressured to actively endorse the abomination of homosexuality. Culture has turned from sinning with a tight fist to celebrating sin we ought to be ashamed of. Great reminders of who is tolerant. This chapter is on the money--- what's coming in your next chapter? Your illustrations are relevant; your comparisons are accurate, your metaphors are powerful. Chapter 3 nearly melted down my computer screen.

A fellow soldier, Gary Strubhar"

Overseas Outreach

P.O. Box 1224, Nampa, ID 83653-1224
Overseasoutreach1998@gmail.com
www.overseasoutreach.com
Phone: 208-284-7425

Our Purpose

IS TO USE THE "MANY
INFALLIBLE PROOFS"
CONCERNING CHRIST,
CREATION, AND THE ACCURACY,
AUTHORITY AND INFALLIBILITY
OF THE BIBLE TO WIN SOULS TO
CHRIST AND TO PREPARE BOLD
WITNESSES FOR JESUS
WHEREVER WE ARE.